TWO LANE GEMS, VOL. 2:

BISON ARE GIANT AND OTHER
OBSERVATIONS FROM AN AMERICAN ROAD TRIP

Also by Theresa L. Goodrich

Two Lane Gems, Vol. 1: Turkeys are Jerks and Other Observations from an American Road Trip

TWO LANE
Gems
Vol. 2

BISON ARE GIANT AND OTHER
OBSERVATIONS FROM AN AMERICAN ROAD TRIP

Love and wanderlust,
Theresa L. Goodrich

THERESA L. GOODRICH

This is a work of creative nonfiction. The events are portrayed to the best of Theresa L. Goodrich's recollection, and while all the places featured in this book are most assuredly real, some of the conversations, names, and identifying details have been tweaked to protect the privacy of the people she encountered.

For more information on the destinations in this book, visit thelocaltourist.com

Author Photograph: Doug White

Cover and Interior Design: Theresa L. Goodrich

Publisher: The Local Tourist

Two Lane Gems, Volume 2: Bison are Giant and Other Observations of an American Road Trip – Theresa L. Goodrich, First Edition

ISBN 978-0-9600495-3-0

CONTENTS

CONTENTS

For Grandma

AND, THEY'RE OFF!

I glared at the dumpster as rain attacked the windshield. This is NOT how I wanted to start our Epic Road Trip. Parked in the lot of a 7-Eleven, staring at a big green hunk of carnage-carrying metal while the wipers slapped and sloshed. We hadn't driven more than two miles before we had to pull over because Mother Nature decided to have a crying jag. Not just any crying. She was weeping her ever-loving-eyes out like a mid-80s Duran Duran fan who just heard the band had split up. THAT kind of crying.

Our exit to I-90 was close enough to smell the I-Pass. I obsessively checked radar and waited. Glared some more. Took a deep breath. Remembered that, even though we were already seven hours behind schedule, we were going to be traveling thousands of miles over the course of more than a month, and a delay of another few minutes, even another few hours, wouldn't matter much in the scheme of things.

It was the second-to-last day of May and my husband, Jim, and I had put everything in storage. We'd timed our road trip to coincide with the end of our lease. No rent = more money to spend on things like gas, places to sleep, and food. We had no idea where we would live when we returned, and for the most part we successfully blocked that uncertainty from our thoughts. That's fairly easy to do when the prospect of a month-long road trip is your reality.

Our loose - very loose - route was to drive until we hit the Pacific Ocean, and then turn around and come back. We had several destinations in mind and had plans to meet lots of Jim's family, but most of the itinerary was just points plotted on a map. A National Park here, a Scenic Byway there, a cattle ranch, horses, a beach, alpacas, a mountain cabin on a lake and my husband's boyhood home.

We had no place to live when we returned, on purpose, and were going on a road trip with very little planned. On purpose.

Who was I and what had I done with control-freak me?

I knew I was out of my comfort zone, but I figured hey - I'd survived the relative lack of planning on our last cross-country trip. In fact, I'd experienced things I never would have if I'd been Ms. Dotted-I-Crossed-T, so why not go for gold and put it all in fate's hands? The no-home thing was a bit of a stretch, but I knew we'd make it work.

Our first destination was one of the few I had scheduled with precision. I'd learned there was a UNESCO City of Literature a few hours away so I reached out to their visitors bureau, and they came back with an index of activities for us to experience. We were supposed to arrive early afternoon, go for a bike ride, explore the Literary Walk, have a nice dinner followed by a relaxing night at our historic inn and then leave early the next day.

The wipers slapped and I glared. Early afternoon had long ago passed. I'd planned one day. One. I'd already miscalculated how long closing up our apartment and packing for this trip would take. When we were supposed to be reading quotes from literary giants embedded in a sidewalk, I had been racing to the bike store to get an adapter bar for my ladies Schwinn so we could carry it however many thousands of miles we'd be traveling. It was already 4 p.m. and here I was constantly refreshing the weather app and willing with all my might for those storm clouds to stop dumping their angst.

And then, the sky lightened, the rain lessened. Angels sang and Mother Nature dried her eyes.

We were on our way.

DAY 1

The drive was uneventful, unless you count what appeared to be funnel clouds off in the distance. Summer in Illinois means there's always a possibility of a tornado, somewhere, but not this time. These formations, while ominous looking, were only a couple of clouds piled up in just the right way. I was grateful that the farms in the distance with their red barns and chartreuse fields would be safe, and our Mississippi River crossing was all blue skies and cotton balls.

Helloooo, Iowa.

Iowa, like most Midwestern states, gets a bad rap. "It's boring." "It's flat." "There's nothing to see." There's even a name for the ennui: flyover country. If you never get off the Interstate, sure. The highway system is designed to be fast, not scenic, and in the plains that means you're taking a straight shot across the state. It's homogeny defined. Gas stations, fast food, the occasional Adult and Fireworks stores (sometimes one and the same), semis and RVs. It's a blur of not-much-to-see-here as you race to your destination. But just like Illinois, Indiana, Nebraska, and yes, even Kansas, if you take an exit, you'll find there's a surprising number of things to see in the Hawkeye State.

Our first exit was Iowa City and our destination, the Brown Street Inn. We parked behind a 1913 Gambrel Cottage-Style Mansion flying both U.S. and rainbow flags from the full-length porch. For the record, I did not know what "Gambrel Cottage-Style Mansion" meant. I've since learned that a Gambrel is a style of roof that looks like a barn. Cottage-style means it looks like a cottage. The word "cottage" implies small. We were staying in an oxymoron.

An artistic, comfortable, tapestry-hung oxymoron.

The sign at the side entrance told us not to let in the cat, so we didn't, and Mark Ruggeberg greeted us with the signature warmth we've come to expect from bed and breakfast proprietors. (Except for one. But he's in another book.) He knew we were late, really, really late, and probably quite hungry, so he gave us the briefest of tours before we left for dinner.

After he kindly let us store our bikes in his garage, we pulled out onto the literally brick-lined street and drove five minutes to the literally-renowned downtown.

Iowa City is a college town, but it's not just any college town. It's the home of the University of Iowa, which is known for, among other attributes, the Iowa Writers' Workshop. Officially monikered the Program for Creative Writing, when it was conceived in 1936, during the Great Depression, it was the first creative writing degree program in the U.S.

By that time, U of I had already established itself as a groundbreaking organization. It was the first public university to open as a coed institution, admitting both men and women in 1855. Remarkably, 41 out of the initial 124 students, a full third of the class, were female. It also opened the first coed medical school, was one of the first to present law degrees to both a white woman (1873) and a black man (1879), and was one of the first to decide it was OK for a black man to play varsity sports (1895).

This is Iowa. A state that's known for feeding the bellies of the world with its productive farms. It also feeds the minds of the world with the words of authors fostered under its cornflower blue skies. The University of Iowa was the first university anywhere to accept creative works on an equal basis with academic research. In essence, they were the first institute of higher learning in the world to realize that a novel or a symphony or an artist's portfolio was every bit as valid as a thesis to represent the sum of a student's learning. On top of that, the University of Iowa created the Master of Fine Arts degree.

All of the above is why Iowa City was the first in the country, and third in the world, to be designated a UNESCO City of Literature.

UNESCO stands for United Nations Educational, Scientific and Cultural Organization, and a summary of its goal is to spread peace through knowledge and understanding. Its Creative Cities Network, of which the City of Literature program is a part, aims to highlight cities with vibrant creative scenes that have a desire to promote cultural diversity.

Iowa City received its designation in 2008, and it's reviewed every four years to make sure it's still offering the programs and resources that made this august body take note.

Short story: it is.

That status is why we were there, but at 7:30 at night after a frustrating day of delays and weather tantrums, all I cared about was a stiff drink and a full dose of comfort food.

We found Clinton Street Social Club, billed as Iowa City's only true gastropub and speakeasy, at 18 1/2 South Clinton Street. Up the stairs we trod until we came upon a wall of whiskey, a dimly lit dining room, a red pool table, and poutine.

Ah, poutine. That all-Canadian comfort food that feels right at home in the heartland of America.

We made the ill-advised choice to share this dish of fried potatoes topped with beef gravy and it's amazing that neither one of us stabbed a fork in the other for taking more than our fair share of its creamy, savory, salty, squeaky goodness. I know Canadians are nice and they've got health care for all and a mighty-fine-looking Prime Minister, but I'm sorely tempted to move north solely for the poutine.

Poutine. Beef gravy crave-worthy poutine.

Or I could just move to Iowa City, eh?

Bonus: there were cheese curds in that poutine. Hallelujah, there were cheese curds. AND a cocktail made with Laphroaig, Aperol, Lillet aperitif wine, Drambuie, and house-made lemon bitters.

Is this heaven?

No, Theresa. It's Iowa.

We split a chicken sandwich and looked at the dessert menu. Although we were ready to curl up in our don't-let-the-cat-in Red Room, Clinton Street Social Club had beignets.

Jim and I met in 2009 right before the holiday season. We had a connection, although neither of us was quite sure what kind of connection that was, and we began sending text messages back and forth. As a professional Christmas caroler, he'd invite me to hear him sing when he had a public gig. Every time he'd invite me, I had something else planned.

Every single time. As we neared Christmas, he sent me one more invitation to hear him sing at the Elysian (now the Waldorf Astoria) Chicago. "They have orange beignets."

It was as charming and decadent as sugar-dusted pastries in a four-star hotel can be. I was smitten.

And I had plans.

This is why we didn't stab each other over poutine. There was something simple and sweet about our courtship. I didn't get my beignets that day, but I ended up with much more, and now we share them any chance we get.

We returned to Brown Street Inn and slipped into bed with fresh chocolate chip cookies and a cup of tea, orange spice for me and raspberry royale for him. It hadn't been the easiest of days, but it turned out OK, and we slept in the comfort of a cottage-style mansion, dreaming of the journey ahead.

Beignets are our thing. Can you blame us?

DAY 2

I woke up a few seconds before my alarm was scheduled to screech. I stretched, made sure I hadn't gotten a stray chocolate chip on the pillow, and scribbled in my journal a bit before we showered, packed up, and headed downstairs.

Breakfast at Brown Street Inn was a communal affair. The sideboard was loaded with assorted breads, hard boiled eggs, and glorious cinnamon pecan rolls. Once we sat down at the large dining room table, a colorful plate of fresh fruit magically appeared next to a crystal bowl of rhubarb jam.

It was delicious, but I expected that. I've stayed in a lot of B&Bs and breakfast has been superb at every one. I love food, so this alone might make me choose this type of lodging over another. But that's not the real reason I enjoy these cozy inns.

It's the people.

That morning we met Will and Susan, who were visiting for his 55th High School Reunion at a nearby town. Dennis was a traveling businessman from Minneapolis who had an Iowa circuit. Miriam from Maine was finishing up a summer session with the Iowa Writers' Workshop. We all exchanged pleasantries and our conversation turned to travel as soon as they learned about our adventure. Will and Susan said we needed to visit Powell's City of Books in Portland. Mark and his partner, Bob Brooks, suggested a visit to Stringtown Grocery in Amish Kalona on our way out of town. Dennis was a bit more philosophical, and we felt like he was in lockstep with the reason we were taking this crazy journey.

"If only people would get out there and meet others, they'd see we're more alike than different," Dennis said.

I wanted to shout "Yes!" It's easy to judge others as a group. When you meet someone, share a cinnamon pecan roll, pass the rhubarb jam, appreciate the hosts who've provided the spread, you've made a connection.

Mark and Bob filtered in and out, commenting occasionally, never once sitting, always the consummate hosts.

"We're going to do this 'til we die," Mark said.

"Could be tomorrow," Bob replied.

I browsed their eclectic art collection. Eclectic is overused, but I'm not sure how else to describe a place that has a pearl-choked dancing pig

in a dress, a meat-grinder coated with a rainbow of beads, and pastoral scenes of rural Iowa, all in the same room. There's a grandfather clock, a gilded framed mirror over the mantel, blown glass sculptures and vases, abstract pieces lining the staircase, and gorgeous tapestries on the floor and the wall. It's chaotic and orderly.

An oxymoron, if you will.

We collected our bikes from the garage and hoisted them back on the rack. Before we headed downtown, I peeked at the house hidden behind a couple of trees at the end of the block. Instead of a sign proclaiming "Kurt Vonnegut, Jr. Wrote Here," there was a sign warning all to stay off the private property. I respected that, but I still stood in the street and stared. This was where the Pulitzer Prize-winner penned parts of *Slaughterhouse Five*. I imagined the click of the keys and wondered what it would be like to step inside.

I didn't stare long, though. One, that would be pretty creepy. I mean, people actually lived there, and I didn't want to be one of *those* tourists. Two, we had to get going. Our campground that night was clear on the other side of the state, and Iowa is pretty wide. (Not as wide as Montana or North Dakota or Oregon, but it still spans a lot of miles.) But first, we had a few things to see.

One of the contributing factors in Iowa City's designation as a City of Literature was their Literary Walk. It's the Hollywood Walk of Fame for authors. Instead of stars, in 2000 - 2001 artist Gregg LeFevre installed bronze panels for each writer that included a quote from the author's body of work. There are 49 in all, including Vonnegut, Raymond Carver, Flannery O'Connor, John Sandford, and Bill Bryson. We strolled, stopped, read; strolled, stopped, read, up and down Iowa Avenue until we'd read them all. Seeing them together illustrated the huge impact this small Midwestern town has had on literature in the last century.

We read the final tribute at the corner of Iowa and Clinton (Tennessee Williams' lament: "We're all of us sentenced to solitary confinement inside our own skins, for life!") and crossed the street to the Old Capitol Building, a beautiful stone structure with a glinting gold dome. Built in 1840, it was the seat of the 29th state's government when it was admitted to the union in 1846. Politicians crafted Iowa's constitution in the building, and the first governor's inauguration was held there. The Old Capitol Building, which is now the centerpiece of the University of Iowa's campus, was also where it was decided the state needed a public university in the first place. That prescient decision, made in 1847, meant U of I had some pretty cool digs when Des Moines became the capital ten years later.

Classes are no longer held inside, but you can still get an education. We entered through the hefty doors and browsed the Old Capitol Museum, which houses the restored Supreme Court and Senate Chambers from the building's days as the seat of government, as well as two rooms with rotating exhibits that emphasize the importance of the humanities. Makes sense, considering the university's history in the subject. We caromed from room to room like we were on a scavenger hunt. Senate Gallery: check. President's Office: check. Five minutes listening to the 1880s Mermod Freres music box: check.

We raced through the museum because, while I'd gained a semblance of calm after our restful night and convivial morning, I was still anxious. Our late start the day before combined with our nomadic state, our loosey-goosey itinerary, and my general need to do everything and see even more fostered a constant rumble of panic. I had to let go of what we didn't get a chance to see and relish what we did.

After a quick stop at Oasis Falafel to pick up a couple of pita sandwiches and a pack of pitas to go, we drove south towards Kalona.

"South?" you ask. "Aren't you supposed to be going west?"

Yes, but we needed to see some Amish about a bug spray.

Mark and Bob swear by Bug Soother and had some on their balcony for Brown Street Inn guests. Once they learned we'd be doing a lot of camping, they sent us to an Amish store south of Iowa City to get some of this magic juice. We pulled into the parking lot of Stringtown Grocery and I turned when I heard clip-clopping along 540th Street SW. Being from the Midwest, that was not my first horse-drawn buggy. It was, however, my first Amish mercantile.

The shelves were stacked with plastic containers, the kind you'd see at a deli, and bags filled with spices, candies, chocolates, flours, sugars, popcorn, and nuts. Even though it was cloudy, the sun filtered through faceted skylights that gave so much ambient light it seemed like Edison had been there. There was a refrigerated section in the back, but that was the only sign of electricity.

We browsed the aisles, amazed at how affordable everything was. I wanted to buy all of the candies and chocolates, most of the spices, and some of the popcorn, but our vehicle was stuffed with everything we needed for a month-and-then-some journey, plus last-minute detritus from our move. We had just enough room for two moon pies, a couple pieces of stick candy, and a bottle of Bug Soother.

Let me tell you about Bug Soother. Mark and Bob were, oh, so right. This stuff is amazing. Mosquitoes hang out around my freckles like my body's an open bar, but I spray this elixir and it's like the bouncer finally decided to do his ever-loving-job and kick their free-loading stingers outta this joint.

AND it smells like vanilla and lemongrass. It's the Yankee Candle of bug sprays.

I've since discovered that you can buy Bug Soother at Amazon and Walmart, but I'd rather pick mine up at an Amish store with a side of moon pie any day.

We left Kalona a little after 1:30 in the afternoon. In my original, overly-enthusiastic itinerary, we would have been on the road by 10am because Iowa has a lot of roadside attractions and I wanted to see as many as possible. Instead, we ate a leisurely breakfast, explored the literary walk and the museum, and bought bug spray.

That's what happens on a road trip. At least, that's what happens when Jim and I go on a road trip. Plans change, and before you know it you're driving through a tallgrass prairie outside of Des Moines at quarter 'til two in the afternoon under blue skies and puffs of white.

We entered the Neal Smith Wildlife Refuge on a gently curved two lane road. "These are Iowa's version of switchbacks," I said, giggling like a toddler who'd just made up a knock-knock joke.

Jim groaned. He does that a lot around me.

Neal Smith Wildlife Refuge

It would seem we have a thing for tallgrass prairies. We've been to Midewin in Illinois, Tallgrass Prairie National Preserve in Kansas, and, now, Neal Smith National Wildlife Refuge in Iowa. All three of them have a mission to restore and reconstruct a portion of what had covered more than 240 million acres of the great plains. Less than one tenth of one percent of that ecosystem remains.

At first glance the prairie looks boring. Just a bunch of waving grass. European settlers called it the Inland Sea and the Great American Desert, and it only took a little over a century to convert the prairies that had existed for thousands of years to farmland. The transition was aided by the near-extinction of the bison and the prairie dog. The two animals worked together to aerate the soil, spread seeds, and generally maintain a natural balance in what was a surprisingly complex environment.

Fire was also necessary for these prairies. To a settler, a farmer, a town, fires are bad. But they're the lifeblood of the prairie, clearing dead plants and adding nitrogen to the soil.

Those three elements - bison, prairie dogs, and fire - became themes of our road trip. The latter was expected. We'd chosen to visit the northwest because we wanted to see how the area had survived after the wildfires of 2017. The bison and prairie dogs were a bit of a surprise, though. We knew after our visit to Wichita Mountains Wildlife Refuge the year before, and to Midewin the year before that, that bison were making a comeback. We just had no idea how extensive the efforts in their resurgence spread.

But I digress.

Di-grass?

In the distance, Jim groans.

ANYWAY.

While a tallgrass prairie restoration and reconstruction may seem like it's all about the plants, Neal Smith Wildlife Refuge is about re-creating an environment that teemed with life. It protects the Walnut Creek Watershed and its prairies, oak savannas, and sedge meadows for the wildlife that depends upon that environment for survival. The refuge is home to bison and elk as well as more than two hundred bird species, about one hundred types of mammals...and "uncounted" thousands of insect species.

Good thing we had our bug spray.

We took the auto tour through the refuge and while we only saw three bison and no elk, the simple beauty of the swaying grasses captivated and calmed.

Speeding through Des Moines' rush hour, we jumped out the other side and got off I-80 to see the road that preceded I-80.

In the early 1900s, when you wanted people to come to your town, you built a road. It was especially effective if that road connected to other towns in a fairly straightforward manner. There was no Federal funding, so you, the resident of the town, did it yourself. In 1910, the people of Dexter, Stuart, Menlo, Casey, and Adair, did just that. They connected their towns and painted the roadside poles white, encouraging drivers to take the "Great White Way." In 1914 it was the first route certified under Iowa's State Highway Commission Rules.

The route went through a myriad of changes, until 2003 when it became the White Pole Road, 26 miles of Iowa personality. Dexter is the "original one-horse town." Stuart is the "Home of 1700 good eggs...and a few stinkers." Adair has a smiling water tower. Driving the White Pole Road is like driving the original alignment of Route 66. When you do it intentionally, there's a presence. You feel connected to the past in a way you never can when you're flying through on an Interstate.

We drove the 26 miles and got back on I-80.

Entrance to White Pole Road

I was done with Iowa.

It's a phrase, I imagine, oft-muttered by many a road warrior. Iowa along I-80 is pretty, in a sameness kind of way. It's lush. Well, it was when we were there, after a heavy rain that painted the fields. But it was so much sameness. Field after field, gentle hill after lone tree after rows of corn. Pastoral, peaceful, graceful, beautiful.

I needed grit and bluffs and crags. This stretch of Iowa was a lullaby, a gorgeous, plentiful lullaby, and all I wanted was a beat that I could dance to.

Or, at the very least, a Volkswagen Beetle spider.

We'd heard that there was such an oddity in Avoca, Iowa, so we pulled off the highway when we saw the town's exit. There was no listing on Google maps, and no sign saying "VW Bug on stilts this way." We stopped at the first gas station we saw, and wouldn't you know it, the cashier's dad was on the Fair board and had taken her up into the metal arachnid when they were installing it. "It's really cool inside," she said, "but nobody knows where it is. They need to move it to the main road. People come here for the spider."

Yep.

As odd things go, this was one of the oddest. There's a cornfield ('cause it's Iowa) and a farm home with big farm equipment and just hanging out is a Volkswagen bug painted all black on eight legs. Talk about roadside kitsch. Except the road is tucked away like a corner in an attic.

Ah. I get it now. Spider. Corner. Clever, Avoca, very clever.

Avoca's Beetle Spider by a corn field

The western fields of Iowa along I-80 are terraced. There's a level plain, a short drop, and then another plain. The drops curve and flow. The system turns the land into a sculpture, molded by farmers turned artists. It's sensual and confounding. How? How long did this take? For miles and miles we passed these terraces, and I remembered that not only did farmers sculpt the land we could see, underneath there were drainage tiles to irrigate the soil. This is the price they paid for turning prairie into farms.

I'd learned during a previous visit to Iowa that those drainage tiles could be a hundred years old and more, installed by hand and horse. The prairies disappeared, but what replaced them produces a disproportionate amount of the nation's food. It was a trade-off, and now there are efforts to find a balance.

We got to the Missouri River and turned north. It was 7:30 when we reached our exit and we still had to pick up propane for our campstove so we could have dinner that night. We had realized at some point in the previous 540 miles that we'd left our tanks in the trunk of our car, which was sitting at my son's house in Illinois. Finally, at our third store, which was obviously the closest to our campground, we found a place that sold those green cylinders.

I hadn't made a lot of plans before we left, but I did have our campsite reserved for this night. Thank goodness. When we pulled up to Blue Lake, an oxbow remnant of the Missouri River's previous meanderings, ours was the only open spot. We unfurled our tent for the first time in more than a year. We finished setting up and the sun was nearly beyond the horizon. The RV-ers three sites down had one final roust with some kids on a speedboat. "Stop skiing! That's so rude!" an RV-er screamed. "How long have you been here? We've been coming here 25 years!" a skier returned. Yada yada yada.

Dinner? We tossed the propane into the Jeep and went to bed.

DAY 3

When we're camping, my body has a very keen awareness of the sunrise. Like clockwork, when it's still dark but the sky starts to lighten in the distance, it decides I have to go to the bathroom NOW. I've learned to keep slip-on shoes next to the air mattress and a flashlight in the tent pocket by the door flap.

I used to think it was the birds getting me up, but the same thing happened in Joshua Tree, where there weren't any early songs.

Nope. Just my body saying GET UP GET UP GET UP YOU NEED TO GET UP NOW WHY ARE YOU ASLEEP GET UP NOW.

Fine. I went to the bathroom. Came back. Drank a perfect cup of camping coffee as, behind the tree line across the lake, orange turned to yellow and ripples hit the shore from the jumping fish and the anglers in boats looking to land them. With the exception of the constant drone from the nearby Interstate (which might have been a contributing factor in my early rising), the morning was peaceful. That droning was also a reminder

of why we prefer two lanes. Only one other camping experience was noisier - and boy, was it ever, but I'll tell you about that later.

Only a couple of other campers were awake. It was easy to tell because this campground had no separation between sites. It was a line of plots of grass marked by posts and gravel drives and the occasional tree. This was not my preferred type of camping, but we weren't there for camping's sake. We were there to see a keelboat.

Our campground was the Lewis and Clark State Park. I should specify that this was the Lewis and Clark State Park in Iowa, because there are *lots* of Lewis and Clark State Parks. Iowa's edition has full-size replicas of the big barge, known as the keelboat, and other boats used on the expedition. They've also got Lizard.

If you want to know anything about Lewis and Clark, go to the state park in Iowa and talk to Lizard. "If anyone ever tells you anything about Meriwether and William's travels, ask them how they heard about it." He has copies of the original journals and gets his facts straight from the explorers themselves.

I asked Lizard, why Lizard? He wouldn't tell us until we'd taken a turn through the museum and came back with a question about the exhibits.

Fair enough.

When we returned to the front desk, Jim asked about the keelboat and Lizard gave us an inside scoop: Even though the explorers' main boat is called the "keelboat" over and over again, and the Iowa state park has a replica of the barge Lewis and Clark used and it's called the Keelboat Display, and their keelboat is mentioned pretty much anywhere you see anything about the explorers, the word *keelboat* doesn't appear in their journals. Meriwether's pre-expedition shopping list mentioned a "keeled boat," and they wrote about other boats as being keel boats, but nowhere do they refer to *their* boat as a keelboat.

Because we did our homework, Lizard gave up the nickname. He told us he's an historian programmer who specializes in the years of 1804 to 1840. His particular avocation is Mountainman camp organizer and Booshway, or head man at the trading post. During reenactments, he would keep his pet iguana on his shoulder. One day, he was talking to a lady and this iguana was sitting as still as could be on top of his head. The lady asked him who his taxidermist was, and at that precise moment the cold-blooded creature turned its head and stuck its tongue out. The lady clutched her skirts and ran across the field, screaming "LIZAAAARRRDDD!!!!" the entire way.

He's been Lizard ever since.

We packed up Jeannie the Jeep, our rented chariot, and continued west, crossing the Missouri River and entering Nebraska, our third state. Shortly after we turned north onto the Lewis and Clark Scenic Byway, Jim got news that we'd been dreading.

His aunt died.

He hadn't seen her in 20 years, and I'd never met her. I was going to, we were supposed to see her, in sixteen days.

We wanted to scrap it all and drive straight to Colfax, Washington. Family said no, don't.

We stopped at Blackbird Scenic Overview. The symbolic earthlodge, representing a dwelling of the Omaha people, overlooks the Missouri River and is a memorial to Chief Blackbird. A couple who'd parked their RV on the side of the road left as we arrived, and then it was just us, the river below, and Jim's memories.

I took pictures of the interpretive signs inside the earthlodge to give him space.

So close. Sixteen days.

We followed US-75 north, stopping in Winnebago to see the Clans Sculpture Garden and Cultural Plaza, a circle of twelve statues with each representing a clan in the Winnebago nation. Further up the byway was an historical marker detailing how the Winnebago were forcibly removed from Minnesota to the Dakota Territory, eventually making their way to the Omaha Reservation, where they bought a piece of that nation's land to make a home of their own. A herd of bison grazed a hundred or so yards away under a grove of trees, which made sense since it was 50 shades of Hades out there.

We turned west on NE20 south of Sioux City, leaving the Lewis and Clark Scenic Byway. Although we would encounter the explorers several times along our journey, we weren't following their path. Our route was even more convoluted than theirs, and for a short part of it we followed in the hoofprints of Doc Middleton, James Jameson, and the Jesse and Frank James Gang.

The Outlaw Trail Scenic Byway is a stretch of 231 miles across north central Nebraska. We drove it from Devil's Nest, a network of deep canyons and canopies of trees that offered the perfect hideaway for the brigands, to the Sandhills, miles and miles of sand dunes anchored with grasses. The latter, an ecoregion that covers a little more than a quarter of the state, was designated a National Natural Landmark in 1984.

I didn't know. I'd driven through Nebraska years ago, and what I

A marsh in Nebraska. Nebraska? Nebraska.

remember from that mindless trek was cornfields. Lots of cornfields. That's how I pictured the state. One. Big. Cornfield. And flat. Oh, my, was it flat. Flatter than my version of Journey at the karaoke bar. Flatter than a crepe. Flatter than a creep flattened by a knockout punch. Flatter than I-80 in Nebraska. Oh, wait.

We drove through marshes and grasslands, over creeks, past shallow lakes, towards green-covered hiccups. There were so many hills and domes it was like Mother Nature had a touch of gas and the Sandhills were what was left, in the most verdant, lush way possible.

(I'll be using that word a lot. Lush, I mean. Not verdant. That would be obnoxious.)

This was Nebraska?

Yes. THIS was Nebraska.

I knew there was more to the Cornhusker State than corn, because a friend of mine wrote a book called *Detour Nebraska*. Within its pages I found one surprise after another, including a 70-foot waterfall near a town called Valentine.

It was all blue skies and sunshine until about an hour out from Smith Falls State Park. There was no foreshadowing. One minute it was a bright shiny afternoon, and the next we were driving towards a shelf cloud and extreme weather warnings were popping up on our GPS. Hail. Flooding. Tornadoes.

Did I mention we'd be camping that night?

"It's going to be OK. It'll blow over. It'll be fine," I muttered to myself with every lightning flash. Would we spend our evening glaring at another

dumpster until the storm passed? This was our third day, and if this kind of weather plagued the whole journey, it was going to be a very long trip.

We neared Smith Falls and learned that we'd been driving between two storm cells, both of which were traveling away from us. Somehow we'd threaded the needle. The retreating sky was like the underbelly of a witch's cauldron. Eye of newt stuff. When we got into the park to see if there were any campsites, the rain had slowed to a drizzle and we could see a hint of sun to the west.

This was the first of our kinda-planned-but-not-really nights. I knew Smith Falls had a campground with a few walk-up sites. There weren't many, but when two huge storm cells blow through right before you pull up in all your "Hi! You gotta spot?" glory, you're more likely to find a home for the night. Ranger Amy got us set up and we followed the rain-rutted road down to the campground.

We parked in the grass at the edge of our riverside spot and unloaded our mud-caked bikes. By the time our campsite was arranged, the sun was in full force. You'd never know there'd been a huge storm barreling through an hour or so before. We took the short hike to the falls, returning in time for the golden hour. A few sites away, a troupe of Boy Scouts settled in, and next to us a family erected a tent that looked like a palace. The Niobrara River flowed by as I seared bacon wrapped filets and sauteed diced potatoes on our campstove.

Another day in the books, we turned in feeling a little more like our road warrior selves, although we still had a ways to go.

DAY 4

Is there anything as supremely peaceful as sitting in a camp chair by a wild and scenic river, sipping a cup of coffee while birds sing and skip from branch to branch on a tree that's a mere two feet away?

For me, that morning, the answer was no.

Nature orchestrated the soundtrack. No constant drone from a nearby highway, no speed boat cutting through the water, no chatter from neighboring campers, although that would come later. I was the first one up, again, and I reveled in the early morning solitude. Gradually, I began to unwind from the tension of the last several weeks. Just under the surface, the knowledge that we had no home poked at my comfort, but I knew we'd find someplace to live and that it would be better than what we'd had before.

In the meantime, I sipped my coffee and watched the water flow.

Smith Falls State Park straddles a portion of the Niobrara River that's been declared a National Wild and Scenic River. If you didn't know there was such a thing, it's probably because less than a quarter of one percent of the nation's rivers have received this designation. Established by President Lyndon Johnson in 1968, the Wild and Scenic Rivers Act preserves free-flowing rivers with clean water that are mostly in their natural state, and that also have shorelines that are fairly easy to reach. Rivers also need to have "outstanding remarkable values." Niobrara's are the quantity of fossils buried in its banks, the largely undisturbed views, and the unique combination of both western and eastern flora and fauna that find a home in this region's microclimates. The surrounding sandhills are semi-arid, but the many canyons that cut through the bluffs are cooler, so much cooler that trees survive here that can't be found anywhere else in the state.

For now.

The land was last sculpted during the Wisconsin Glaciation around 10,000 years ago. A few tree species from that colder era remain in the microclimates within those canyons, including the paper birch. Those species are threatened. Increasing temperatures due to climate change have kept the trees from reproducing, and the ones that remain are dying. We noticed several fallen paper birches on our return walk to the falls that morning. Their white bark, peeling like curled parchment marred by slashes of brown, was striking and we couldn't miss them discarded on the canyon floor.

We followed the boardwalk that protected the fragile environment. It was before 9am and for a while we were the only people in the canyon. The falls, the tallest in the state, were an antidote to the previous days, weeks, and months. We inhaled the spray. We kissed and I said "yes." Jim had proposed by a waterfall, so whenever we're near one I have the urge to let him know I'd still say yes.

(I should probably warn you now that we saw a LOT of waterfalls on this trip.)

Amy, the Park Ranger we'd met the previous evening, strolled up the boardwalk. She told us she was off that day, but she liked hiking out to the falls before anyone else was there because it's so peaceful. (Sorry, Amy!) She lived in the middle of nowhere, with no cell service, so close that when she first moved in she thought she could hear the falls from her house. "My family thinks I'm crazy," she said, but as we left her to her solitude and returned to camp, I wasn't so sure. She just might have the right idea.

Fifteen minutes west of Smith Falls State Park is Fort Niobrara National Wildlife Refuge. Before entering, we pulled off at an overlook and drank in the sight of the transition from wooded canyons to flat grasslands. After the rain from the night before, the expanse before us was a thousand hues of green. You'd never know there used to be an actual military base down there, but then again, it had been gone for more than a century.

The U.S. government established Fort Niobrara in 1879 to protect white homesteaders and keep the peace, which to them meant keeping the Lakota on their reservation lands seven miles to the north. A few years later, the railroad came through and brought settlers who established the town of Valentine to the west. With up to 500 soldiers, the fort was a lively place until the Spanish-American and Philippine-American Wars pulled men to those conflicts, dropping the population to about 100. In 1902, the segregated black 25th Army Regiment came back from the Philippines and stayed in this remote Nebraskan fort for the next four years. The population grew to nearly 800 men, but that wasn't enough to keep the fort open. By 1906 those Buffalo Soldiers were shuttled to Brownsville, Texas. For the

Fort Niobrara National Wildlife Refuge

next five years, the Quartermaster and his men supplied horses to the army from the fort. By 1912, they were gone, too. President Roosevelt ordered the buildings razed and set aside the land as a game preserve, making Fort Niobrara National Wildlife Refuge the 27th in a system which now has more than 550 preserves.

We entered the refuge itself and kept our eyes peeled for bison and elk. We didn't see either of those giant mammals, but we did see our first prairie dog town.

Our first prairie dog sighting!

Prairie dogs may be a vital part of the plains ecosystem, but they're also gosh-darn cute. They'd pop up, take a look around, scurry to another hole and dive in. The wind was tearing across the flat lands so we couldn't hear them chirping, but we'd catch a glimpse of movement as they reared up on their hind legs or twitched this way or that before scampering across the gravel drive. It's a wonder we didn't run over the little buggers.

We left Fort Niobrara and followed the Outlaw Trail Scenic Byway to its terminus in Valentine. After we got a few gallons of gas - but not enough - we turned north for South Dakota. We were going to the Badlands.

The change from Nebraska to South Dakota was so subtle we didn't even notice until we realized we were on reservation land. "We're in South Dakota!" I grinned. I'd never been in the state before. It was one of many firsts for me on this trip.

We drove north through Rosebud Indian Reservation until we got to Mission and turned west. We'd passed a gas station, but prices seemed high so I suggested we skip it. Surely there would be another gas station between where we were and Badlands National Park.

You'd think I'd never been on a road trip before.

There are two cardinal rules of road trips: go to the bathroom before you have to, and never pass a gas station when you're below half a tank in the middle of a place with no cell service. It was not my first rodeo, yet here we were coasting down hills because the distance-to-empty was precipitously low.

Jim watched the fuel gauge and I watched the scenery. We entered the Pine Ridge Reservation and for the first time in more than 24 hours saw arable land. In the Midwest it's rare to drive more than an hour or two without seeing a field, a farm, or a town. Technically, South Dakota is the Midwest, but it certainly didn't feel like it. I knew from that point on, until we made our way back and reached Minnesota, the sight of fields would be more of a rarity than a certainty. This was unknown territory and I gazed out the window in wonder.

I breathed a sigh of relief when we pulled into Wanblee's gas station. Jim didn't say a word, but then again, he knew he didn't have to. I wasn't about to make that mistake twice. We filled up again in Interior, South Dakota, at Cowboy Corner, a relic of a station with mechanical gas pumps, a painted horse, and the shell of a covered wagon. In the background, the spine of the Badlands beckoned.

Fourth day. Fourth state. Third night camping.

Maybe.

The Ben Reifel Visitor Center at the Interior entrance to Badlands National Park was a madhouse. We'd already picked up our National Parks Access Pass, which would get us into that park and all future ones for a year, and now we needed to find a place to sleep for the night. We dodged Junior Rangers and families, finally making our way to the counter. I asked about campsites and the Ranger pulled back and eyed me like I was all sorts of crazy. "Oh, they've been filling up every night." He looked at the clock. 4 pm. "They're probably all gone by now."

Our plan had been to camp at Sage Creek Campground, which was free and first come, first served. However, that was clear across the park and he told us it would take at least an hour to get there. We tried Cedar Pass Campground, since it was right there. Pulled up behind an RV. An RV that took the last spot.

Crap crap crappity crap.

We turned around and drove towards the other end of the park. I don't think I can describe how frustrating it was to take one of the most scenic drives in the country and not stop at a single overlook or pull-out. Priorities. If we found a place to sleep, we'd have time to drive the Badlands Loop State Scenic Byway. For now, we needed to get to Sage Creek.

Despite my tension, as we neared the campground I could see where it got its name. The landscape had migrated from bluffs and spires to calming sage-colored ripples. We turned off the main road and down into a relatively flat plain filled with bison and tents.

So many tents.

The campground itself was one big oval. There were a few sheltered picnic tables, some tables without any cover, and a couple of pit toilets on opposite sides of the oval from each other. It was basically just a field, and campers staked their claim wherever they could find an open spot. It wasn't quite a free-for-all, though. There's a code among campers, one that includes allowing a certain amount of space between you and your neighbor.

We circled twice, finally deciding that a space we weren't sure about really did have enough room for our tent. Other hopeful campers circled after us, and we realized we'd gotten the last spot.

It wasn't the first time we'd underestimate the popularity of a place,

Sage Creek Campground - Complete with wandering bison

nor the last time we'd luck into the last place available to sleep for the night.

What I've failed to mention is that outside that oval, a whole herd of bison was milling about as casually as a bunch of cows along the side of the road. But these weren't cows. They were bison. Those HUGE GIGANTIC TRUCKS of the animal kingdom. The ones they warn you about with big signs. "Stay away," they say. "These are wild animals and they can kill you," they say. And then they put a campground IN THE MIDDLE OF THE BISON.

We gamely attempted to ignore the beasts while we set up camp and made dinner. As we dined on Wisconsin brats and bagged salad, we noticed a ranger stopping to talk to each camper before approaching our table. She was inviting everyone to the evening program, where she'd be demonstrating how to throw an atlatl.

My eyes bugged out and I scarfed my brat. Jim smirked and said something along the lines of "So, you want to go see this?" and I replied "YES YES YES I WANT TO SEE THIS!"

Before you think I'm totally off my rocker, I'd read about atlatls in my teens. I think the first time was in Jean Auel's *Earth's Children* book series. Anyway, these spear throwers were one of the first hunting tools used by humans, as in 30,000-years-ago first tools. This ingenious invention could propel a dart more than the length of a football field. Most importantly, it could pierce the thick hide of a bison.

We made our way across the campground, dodging bison pies

How to use an atlatl - Complete with heckling prairie dog

along the way. Kathleen the Ranger had already begun her demonstration, explaining the physics of the instrument to the growing crowd. Kids stood in front and we all followed along with rapt attention, distracted only by a heckling prairie dog that chirped incessantly anytime she spoke.

After her demonstration, we threaded a path back through the minefield of giant piles of dried poop and jumped in our car. We were in the Badlands and we were *going* to see the sunset. Driving back along the main road, we figured we'd pull over at one of the many overlooks we'd passed in our rush to get to the campground. Most of the road in that part of the park was on the rim, so we knew there wouldn't be a bad place to stop.

Unless we had to because there was a giant bison in the middle of the road.

I realize that "giant" and "bison" are redundant, but I feel the sheer size of these creatures needs to be emphasized. Often. They. Are. Giant.

A line of cars coming the other direction stopped as the beast sauntered a few steps, turned a bit, strolled a few more, and began loping towards us. Oh crap oh crap oh crap. Jim backed up slowly. Did you know that bison can run up to 40 mph? That's as fast as a horse, but these suckers are the biggest mammals in North America and have an average weight of 1,400 pounds. Our SUV, our suddenly petite Jeep Cherokee, was perched

on the spine of a butte and that charging animal had more than enough power to push us over the edge. The beast slowed, and as we looked to our right we saw the reason for his aggression.

He had a friend, and she was stranded on the side of the road all by herself.

When we'd backed up far enough (thank goodness there were few cars behind us and they backed up, too), Mr. gathered up Mrs. and they loped across the road to the other side. Exhaling, we drove until the next overlook and watched a glorious sunset over a wild and majestic land.

DAY 5

I've had a lot of early morning visitors while camping. Deer. A roadrunner. Rabbits. Turkeys (jerks). But, until this morning, never in my life have I stepped out of the tent and almost immediately come nose to snout with a creature as tall as our SUV and strong enough to smush me with one prairie-tearing hoof.

The sun edged over the ridge and I heard magpies for the first time. I listened, blinked, and there he was. "Nose to snout" might be a slight exaggeration, but not by much. We'd staked our tent a few feet from Jeannie the Jeep and on the other side of the road a bison was munching his way around the campground. Another early-riser and I stood on the safe side of our respective vehicles and marveled at the sheer size of this creature. Here and there, more bison were making their way through the dew-covered grass, ripping it out of the ground with their massive jaws. As the morning progressed, one strolled up to a picnic table and used it to scratch an itch. Another stopped right next to a tent and dropped a pile of poop. All of this was within swatting distance of people who were advised by the signs next

to the pit toilets to keep 100 yards away from these animals.

It was surreal and frightening, yet peaceful. Another oxymoron.

The campground began to awaken. I noticed a couple of women next to us had a bike rack similar to ours on the back of their car, and I watched as they popped the trunk - with the bike rack still attached.

Three nights in a row we'd removed our bike rack so we could get into the back of our vehicle for our camping equipment, only to have to put it back on the next morning, fighting to make sure it was stable enough to handle the drive.

You'd think two fairly intelligent people would realize that if the bike rack is attached snugly enough to keep from falling off when you're driving on bumpy roads or at speeds up to 75 - 80 mph, that it might possibly be secured snugly enough to stay in place when you open the trunk.

I don't know who those two ladies were, but I thank them. There's no telling how long it would have taken us to realize that we could leave the darn thing on. When you camp as much as we did on this trip, mostly one night at a time, having one less task, and an onerous one at that, is a HUGE deal.

Jim was up by seven and we were at our first overlook, sans bike rack, by eight. We'd decided to get up and go and would pack up the site after we'd explored.

"That's distracting," he said.

"What?"

"I can see out the rear window."

It felt a little odd to leave our stuff in an open field where bison roamed and pooped willy-nilly, but we were anxious to actually see these Badlands beyond our brief sojourn the night before.

The length of time it takes to drive from Sage Creek Campground to the entrance of Badlands National Park while stopping at every single overlook is three hours, give or take a few minutes. This allows time to read each wayside exhibit, take innumerable photos of prairie dogs, wait out the tour bus throng when you have the misfortune of reaching an overlook at the same time one is present, and stare in slack-jawed awe at each serrated, striated, stupefying view.

The landscape is a lesson in geology. Bands of color represent the epochs, from the compressed ancient seabed that makes up the nearly-black Pierre Shale, through the fossil soil of the yellow mounds, to the light gray volcanic ash spires of the Sharps Formation. When your eyes roam the horizon you see lines that cut straight through each peak like a printer that's running out of ink.

Left - Badlands; Top - prairie dog!; Bottom - goats!

Left - more Badlands! Top - yellow mounds; Bottom - taking the back road

It's a harsh land, yet somehow humans have lived in this environment for more than 11,000 years.

The Lakota, the last semi-nomadic peoples to live here, called it *mako sica*, or "land bad." They survived by hunting bison on horseback and using everything they could from the animal. Then French fur trappers came, followed by American soldiers, miners, and settlers. The cultures fought desperately for a stake in what each considered home. On December 24, 1890, Chief Big Foot, despite being ill with pneumonia, led 350 of his people through the Badlands to escape the United States Army. Their retreat ended five days later and 50-some miles to the south at Wounded Knee. The Army slaughtered nearly 200 native men, women, and children that day, and the free roaming of the Lakota Sioux ended once and for all.

Since the passage of the Homesteaders Act in 1862, settlers had been steadily arriving, trying to make their own way in this unforgiving environment. It was rough going. They created a checkerboard pattern on a land that didn't play games. Their 160-acre stakes became known as "Starvation Claims," and they lived in tar paper shacks and burned cow chips for fuel. Most of them didn't last. To put it into perspective, today's ranchers in this area of South Dakota need thousands of acres and heavy equipment to survive. As we looked over a land ill-suited for agriculture, I could only imagine the fortitude required to stay and make a life.

We parked in the crowded lot of Burns Basin Overlook and stepped up the boardwalk, passing a "Beware of Rattlesnakes" sign. Along the way to the top, a snarl of tourists hunched in a semicircle. As we approached, we could hear the rattle. At the top of the walk the tour guide fretted with her hands covering her mouth. "It'll strike!" she said, as her charges leaned closer to get a picture. I confess; I probably got a little closer than I should have, but it was my first rattlesnake in the wild and there were people in front of me, so I figured I didn't have to be faster than the snake...

At the top of the overlook the boardwalk expanded to provide more room to view the panorama. We oohed and aahed, then headed back to Jeannie and noticed a couple hiking where there was no path. An Aussie gent from the tour bus pointed at them *Invasion of the Body Snatchers-*style.

"They're degrading the surface!" he shrieked. "They're degrading the surface!"

His outraged hue and cry became our all-purpose mantra any time in the future we saw people going where they weren't supposed to go. Group walking right by the 'Do not walk here' warning? "They're degrading the surface!" Lady making a snow-angel next to a sign telling her to stay on the sidewalk? "She's degrading the surface!" Somebody cutting in front of a line of cars at the exit? "He's degrading the surface!"

You get the point.

We continued toward the entrance of the park. At some overlooks, the buttes melted into the plains. At others, the spires' permanence seemed undeniable, even though geologists estimate they'll all be gone in another 500,000 years. At our last stop, the Fossil Exhibit Trail, we glimpsed the morbid sense of humor of the National Park Service. One sign detailed how mammals were "Dying to become a fossil." The Welcome sign to the short trail informed us that animals could Move, Adapt, or Die, with a picture of a dead oreodont, its legs straight up in the air, illustrating the last option.

Have I mentioned how much I love our National Park Service?

We took the long-way-around-shortcut back to the campground through Buffalo Gap National Grassland. It didn't save us any time, but we got to drive faster, and anyone who's dealt with traffic and short mileage vs. clear lanes and longer distance will choose the latter every time. Thankfully, our tent and bikes were upright and pie-free, so we loaded up for our next destination.

When I began talking about this trip and the potential route we'd take, a friend of mine from high school told me she had relatives along the way. Her Great Aunt Alice had lived in New York, but then a cowboy - a literal cowboy - came to town, swept that city girl off her feet and brought her out west, and she's been there ever since. My friend put me in touch with her Aunt's son Paul and daughter-in-law Linda, and that's how we ended up on a cattle ranch near Whitewood, South Dakota.

None of us were sure what to expect. All they knew was that a member of their family had friends coming through, and all we knew was that a friend had family in a place we'd be traveling.

Little did we guess that we'd be staying with the descendants of homesteaders. Paul's grandfather came out from Ohio in the late 1870s. When he got to Bismarck by rail, he sent his stuff south on a bull train of ox-drawn wagons. He walked, and even though the "Indians wouldn't let the white man cross" in Pierre, he somehow made his way west and claimed a homestead. That original ranch was quite a ways east of Sturgis, but after the blizzard of 1949, Paul's dad, Ray, vowed that he wasn't going to stay another winter on the prairie. That year, "It started snowing January 1 and Dad didn't see the ground until mid-May."

That'd do it.

Ray picked up and moved to Whitewood. Shortly after that, he took a fateful trip to New York City and met an organist named Alice.

Paul was working when we got there, so Linda took us on a tour of their ranch. It's extensive, but don't ask how many head they own. I did, and it was like I'd asked how much money they had in the bank. As a matter of fact, it was *exactly* like that. You don't ask farmers how many acres they own, and you don't ask ranchers how big their herd is. In this family's case, both subjects were off-limits, since they raise cattle and grow the feed that sustains them. This is more economical than buying the feed, but it also means they never get a vacation.

Most ranchers get a break during the summer, and most farmers get a break in the winter. By doing both, this family has no down-time, and they're OK with that.

We met some of the "girls," as Linda called the cows, and Jim noticed there was one red lady in the sea of black angus. They were a bit surprised when she was born with that color hide, but the neighboring ranch had red

"The girls," with one rogue redhead in the back

angus, so they figured somebody must've "jumped the fence." I thought I might be a little uncomfortable seeing the cows, but they seemed, I don't know, happy. Later I found out that Paul and Linda are big followers of Temple Grandin, who transformed the world of cattle care, and they designed their system based on her guidelines.

Before heading back to the house for dinner with Paul, their two sons, and their daughter Kay, a literal Rodeo Queen, Linda took us to their church in Nisland. Built in 1930 as Peace Evangelical Lutheran Church, the exterior is a simple white clapboard building with a tall spire. It's an architectural style you'll see frequently in places where Germans emigrated, and Nisland's population was so German services were only conducted in their native language until 1941. The interior's pulpit and intricate altar reminded me of the Lutheran church my grandparents attended in Lafayette, Indiana. Because of the smaller size of the congregation in South Dakota, the church in Nisland went through several changes. In the mid-70s the church joined Village Missions, a non-denominational organization that supports churches in rural areas. As of 2018 they were in more than 230 North American communities.

Nisland Independend Community Church

Dinner that night was pork (not beef), potato salad, and watermelon, served with iced tea and water next to family photos and a box of Gideon bibles. I sat across from Alice and could see why a rancher would want to take the feisty New Yorker home with him. Paul told stories and Linda served cake. This was the postcard picture of rural America, a romanticized Norman Rockwell-painting made real.

Their gracious hospitality gave us a glimpse into a different way of life than I'd experienced, and an even greater appreciation for the people who grow and nurture our food.

None of us had been sure what to expect, but as Jim and I went to bed, we thought it had turned out all right.

DAY 6

We left the next morning after a meal of strawberries and cream, hard-boiled eggs, and homemade raspberry muffins. Before breakfast, we didn't know where we'd be that day, except for a drive through Deadwood and a landing point somewhere in the vicinity of Mount Rushmore. After breakfast, we had a fistful of destinations and a potential campground.

It was Day 6 and I finally felt comfortable with our intentionally unintentional itinerary. While we didn't have a lot of specifics planned, we weren't exactly throwing a dart at a map to choose our next location. I had stuck pins in our overnight spots - they just weren't precisely placed. I'm sure part of this lack of finite planning was to test my capacity for uncertainty, but the main reason was that I truly believed that through luck, optimism, and trusting in people, we'd have unexpected experiences that would make our lives richer and introduce us to areas we'd never see with a script.

(Spoiler alert: we did.)

Our first destination of the day was Bear Butte State Park. We'd seen this formation in the distance as soon as we neared Whitewood. It's an isolated peak that juts 1,200 feet from the earth like a pyramid in the desert. It's easy to see why it's a sacred place to the Lakota and Cheyenne. No matter where we drove, its presence followed us like the eye of Sauron, albeit with a much more beneficent outlook.

To the Lakota, it's *Mato Paha*, or Bear Mountain. The Cheyenne call it Noahvose. Both nations consider it a place of pilgrimage for meditation and peace, leaving prayer cloths and bundles tied to tree branches.

"Butte" is a misnomer. A butte, strictly speaking, is formed by erosion. Bear Butte, on the other hand, is the result of an intrusion known as a *laccolith* (you'll see this word again). Magma lurched to the surface, pushing the rock above it higher. Instead of breaking through, like a volcano, the magma cooled and became igneous rock. Then erosion removed the outer sedimentary layers, leaving behind a peak that has been a gathering place for humans for 10,000 years.

In 1857, leaders from several tribal nations, including Red Cloud, Crazy Horse, and Sitting Bull, met at Bear Butte to discuss the threat of

Bear Butte

the white man and his encroachment on their lands. They were right to be concerned. By 1868, the Treaty of Fort Laramie established the Great Sioux Reservation, protecting land that encompassed the Black Hills, but it lasted all of six years. George Armstrong Custer broke the treaty in 1874 when he led an expedition to the area and confirmed rumors that there was gold in them thar hills. After that, nothing could stop the influx of miners and settlers wanting their piece of the American dream. It was so egregious that in 1980, the U.S. Supreme Court ruled that the government had illegally taken the land and awarded the Lakota Sioux a settlement of $120.5 million, which by 2017 had compounded to over $1.4 billion dollars. They refuse to take the money, though, because they want their land back. They believe that accepting the funds would constitute selling the Black Hills, and that is not an option.

Without time to explore the park, we turned around at the cattle guard marking the entrance and made our way to Fort Meade, a mere three miles from Bear Butte. The fort was built in 1878 to protect white settlers from the Sioux. This was ten years after the U.S. government had signed a treaty which prohibited travel and settlement by whites on the Great Sioux Reservation, of which that land was part.

It's hard to reconcile this episode in American history. The family we'd just stayed with was descended from homesteaders, those same homesteaders that moved onto land that was supposed to belong to others, although the treaty had already been broken before their ancestor had arrived. On a macro level it's black and white. Treaties were made and broken as easily as putting crystal in a china cabinet and then dumping the whole thing, over and over. On a micro level, it's one person trying to make a better life and another trying to keep a life he loves.

When we got to Fort Meade there were soldiers running drills. It felt odd to be able to drive right up and park next to active military training, but the South Dakota National Guard lives there and it's an Army National Guard Officer Candidate School. We arrived too early to enter the on-site museum, so we read the historical marker about the fort's status as the home of the National Anthem. In 1892, Post Commander Colonel Caleb Carlton felt the need for a National Air, so at his wife's suggestion, he began requiring that the "Star Spangled Banner" be played at every retreat and at the end of every concert. He also wanted to "enforce respect for the flag," so he made the men remove their hats and told everyone they needed to stand when the colors passed them. Others didn't immediately catch on to the idea, and it wasn't presented to Congress until 1918 - 26 years later. After five failed attempts to pass a bill making the Star Spangled Banner the National Anthem, Congress finally made it official in 1931.

The National Anthem started at Fort Meade

It wasn't even 9 in the morning and my head was spinning, so we went to McDonald's. Don't judge - they had free wi-fi.
(Tip: EVERY McDonald's has free wi-fi.)

It was now Monday and we'd been on the road for almost a week, and while we pretty much had things in order, we still needed to check in occasionally. Jim was already getting bookings for the caroling season. I had an immensely capable editor in place for The Local Tourist, but sometimes I didn't give her all the information she needed. So, we stopped at McDonald's, ordered a couple of sodas, and mainlined caffeine and the Internet for about an hour.

And then, we drank beer, ate pizza, and bought truffles from a chipmunk.

Welcome to Deadwood.

I know, I know. Deadwood is all about the Gold Rush and Wild Bill Hickok and shoot-outs, etc etc etc. It's also a couple of blocks of Disney-esque storefronts with casinos in every other window. While I'm sure there's lots to see, at that moment I was content to skip another history lesson and drink some beer. Fortunately, there was a brewery along Main Street, so we ordered a flight of beer, a pizza from the counter next door, and let the drama fade. On the way out we filled up my fancy new pressurized growler. I was so excited about this thing I'd ordered a box of ten replacement CO_2 cartridges for the trip, and two had come with it in the first place. (Believe it or not, I did not use them all, although I gave it the good ol' road trip try.)

On the way out of town we pulled over at a white brick building with

a wind-up van to the side and a huge bobble-headed chipmunk out front. Before we left the cattle ranch that morning (was it only that morning?), Miss Rodeo Queen had told us about this tasty place for hand-dipped chocolates, so we knew we had to visit Chubby Chipmunk. Oh, how we wanted to dig into every truffle behind the glass, but we settled on four to go and went on our merry way.

One of the many suggestions Paul had offered at breakfast was a campground near Mount Rushmore called Horse Thief. We plugged it into our GPS and arrived at Horse Thief Campground and RV Resort. While it looked fine, and their on-site store was stocked with all sorts of goodies like sunscreen, firewood, and 20-year-old DVDs, this was not the Horse Thief we were looking for. The place we wanted was on a lake and had no such things as electricity and showers. We didn't mind the detour, though; it was a lovely afternoon and a gorgeous drive through ponderosa pines.

We found *our* Horse Thief, and after circling the campground a couple of times to see what was available, picked a large spot that was mostly shaded with sun filtering through the canopy. I could see settling in for a week, it was so perfect. Fellow campers occupied a few other spots, but for the most part it was just us and Mother Nature, and she was in fine fettle that day.

This was our kind of camping. A scenic spot in the woods and people far enough away that we could feel secluded, without being all alone in the wilderness. We were happy to find it, but no sooner did we get set up than we had to turn around again and go back the way we'd just come, including passing the *other* Horse Thief Campground. Our goal was to cut through Custer State Park by taking Needles Highway to Iron Mountain Road and end up at Mount Rushmore in time for their evening program.

Or, as some might call it, the Essential Black Hills Checklist.

Paul had provided these and other stops before we left. He knew Mount Rushmore was our destination, so he told us we had to drive Needles Highway and Iron Mountain. Those two drives are part of the Peter Norbeck Scenic Byway, which is one of the most scenic drives in the country, so if I'd done a modicum of research I would have found them. But what I might not have found was the direction we should take to get the most spectacular views.

And oh, my, were those views spectacular.

It was late in the afternoon when we left the campground. Fortunately, being June, the sun wouldn't set for many hours. We needed the sunlight. Not wanted. *Needed.*

Completed in 1922, the Needles Highway was the impossible road. At the time, nobody believed it could be built. Peter Norbeck thought differently. A South Dakota State Senator, then Governor, then U.S. Senator, he thought it would be great to put a scenic drive through granite spires in the middle of the Black Hills. He also thought having a bunch of faces carved into the side of a mountain would be cool, and if you're going to do that, then why not build another impossible road with spirals that would put a modern-day roller coaster to shame.

I think I would've liked this guy.

We approached the first of his impossible roads and began the winding trek. It didn't take too long before we encountered our first one-lane tunnel. It was nail-biting narrow, a slight ten-and-a-half feet wide. Fortunately, it was also short, and we were out of it and into our next hairpin turn faster than I could say "watch the mirrors!" Groves of Ponderosa pines and paper birch, which thrive in this environment, lined the asphalt in between outcroppings of granite. The sky above this impossible road was an impossible blue, and it seemed impossible that this land was real.

After passing a sign for another one-lane tunnel, we rounded a bend and entered a land of wizardry and make-believe. We were on a road that shouldn't be. There were parking spaces in between gray-granite peaks, and we got out to look at a valley filled with tall, tall trees and a wall of melded spires on the other side. It was like somebody took flaking shale, bleached it, and set it on end. Above us, the blue peeked through a needle-eye-shaped opening in one of the tallest peaks. Back in Jeannie the Jeep, we threaded the Needles Eye Tunnel. Creating this tunnel was sheer hubris. "I want the road to go there," so they blasted a hole in the granite. All of eight feet four inches wide and twelve feet tall, it's not for the distracted driver, or for anyone who parks like they're docking a boat. Our Jeep was six feet three inches wide, so we had a whopping foot and half-an-inch clearance on either side.

We squeezed through with no scrapes or bumps and followed the narrow road, wending and winding our way through the spires. We pulled off to gaze over the tops of the black hills. Hidden beneath the granite and pines were reserves of mica, feldspar, and gold, the gold that drove those early settlers to travel a harsh land and dig for riches. Driving through, I was grateful that Peter Norbeck believed the riches were above ground, too, and should be there for everyone.

The Senator had ridden a horse through the Needles, so named because of the pointy formations, in 1920 to map out his road. What others said was impossible, engineer Scovel Johnson said could be done,

The Black Hills of South Dakota

"if you furnish me with enough dynamite." It took two years and 150,000 pounds of the blasting powder, but they did it. They weren't finished yet, however. Once Norbeck had convinced Congress to provide funding for Mount Rushmore, he wanted another road, one that would be fitting for the monument. So, he got back on his horse, this time with C.C. Gideon, the Superintendent for Custer State Park, and they mapped out a route that would give the carved Presidents their due.

Gideon designed Iron Mountain Road so that the exit from each of the three tunnels would frame the monument. To do this, the road turns like a corkscrew on what are called Pigtail Bridges. Our host from the night before had mentioned these "pigtails," but it's hard to picture them until you're actually driving; turning and turning and turning until you get to another narrow tunnel, come out the other side, and get your first glimpse of Mount Rushmore. And then another. And then another. It's ingenuous and awe-inspiring. Or, to put it the way I did as we pulled out of the Scovel Johnson Tunnel, "COOL!"

Despite being nearly seven at night, every lane to get into Mount Rushmore was backed up. We were all there to see the Evening Lighting Ceremony. We paid our $10 parking fee, which would be good for an entire year, and followed the attendants' directions to the parking structure.

We'd seen the heads in the distance, but that first sight of their faces just above the multi-arched gateway was monumental. Mount Rushmore had never been a bucket list item for me. I knew I wanted to see it, but it wasn't like my desire to visit Yellowstone or Crater Lake, so I was taken aback by my visceral reaction.

And this was before we read a sign outside the cafe proclaiming that Thomas Jefferson authored the first recipe for ice cream in America.

We ordered a bison burger and a scoop of TJ's Vanilla and sat outside in the courtyard, listening to the symphony of languages swirling around us. A yellow-bellied marmot caused some excitement when he neared the patio and several of us jumped up to get a photo, but all I got was a really good picture of grass.

That's OK. I was there for the Presidents.

Dusk came quickly, and after a quick walk under their noses along the Presidential Trail, we returned to the amphitheater and took a spot at the top of the stairs. Rows of benches descended to the stage, and although we were there before the ceremony began, the entire place was full. Above, yellow light bathed the faces of George Washington, Thomas Jefferson, Theodore Roosevelt, and Abraham Lincoln. Below, a Ranger presented a brief history followed by a film that explained why sculptor Gutzon Borglum selected those four specific Presidents.

Including Washington was practically a requirement. The first president laid the foundation for the democracy, and that's why his face is the most prominent. Lincoln's role in ending slavery and preserving the union made his selection obvious, too. Not only was Jefferson the principal author of the Declaration of Independence, his Louisiana Purchase doubled the country's size. Roosevelt stood up for the common laborer by busting corporate monopolies and he connected east and west through the Panama Canal. Combined, those two achievements represented development to Borglum. It probably didn't hurt that Roosevelt also established the United States Forest Service and a total of 51 Federal Bird Reserves. Norbeck, the man responsible for making sure Mount Rushmore happened in the first place, was a like-minded conservationist who'd done for his home state what Roosevelt had done for the country.

After the film, the Ranger invited active members of the military and veterans to join him on stage, and everyone in the crowd stood, honored them, and thanked them for their service.

It was profoundly moving, stirring patriotism and pride in my country. This Shrine of Democracy, as Mount Rushmore is known, exemplifies the best of what America can be and, hopefully, aspires to be.

We left knowing that we'd return in the morning to spend more time at this unexpectedly moving memorial. Fortunately, our campground was a short jaunt on a less demanding road than we'd driven earlier. By 10:15 we were on our air mattress eating truffles. I was worn enough I'd even forgotten about the beer.

Tomorrow. I could drink it tomorrow.

DAY 7

A fine yellow dust covered everything. Jeannie the Jeep, the picnic table, our bikes, us. EVERYTHING. Mrs. Camp Host, a squat, gruff older lady driving a golf cart, pulled the tag from the post at the end of our campsite so new campers would know it was open. "It's the pollen," she huffed. "That lake turns yellow. You can't hardly breathe."

"Oh, wow," I commiserated, not sure what else to say.

"Eh, it gets better." She looked around. "It's worth it."

And she was off on her appointed rounds.

We finished the last of our Wisconsin brats (they'd been frozen when we started and we had a *really* good cooler) with a side of scrambled eggs and pita bread. We took a quick spin around the campground on our bikes, primarily to justify carting them for the past fourteen hundred miles. We also wanted to drink in a little more piney woods before resuming our journey. We rode by a dad reading in the shade while his young daughters played in the lake. A couple packed up their two-person tent, and I thought how tiny it seemed compared to our six-person instant-tent behemoth. But

hey - Jim could set up and break down in five minutes or less, and when you're camping one night at a time, that's a big deal. Plus, we're old. Older than they were, anyway.

Out of six nights, we'd camped four. Not only did we still enjoy it; we still loved it. Plus, because we chose to camp, our trip back to Mount Rushmore that morning would take just twenty minutes.

We got our first glimpse of the Memorial when we sighted Washington's profile from the west. When we arrived at the gate, the attendant greeted us with "Hello, Illinois!" and a "Welcome back, sir!" after noticing our parking pass from the night before. We parked, a little closer this time, and identified license plates as we walked to the entrance. Alabama. Wisconsin. New Mexico. Nebraska (lots of those). Missouri. Illinois. California. Washington. People drove from all over the country to see this Shrine of Democracy, and why wouldn't they? It's a place of hope and higher ideals, ideals exemplified by those 60-foot faces. We didn't spend a lot of time there, but it was worth returning so we could get another look in the bright morning sun.

Half an hour from Mount Rushmore is the Black Hills' other

The Faces of Liberty

64

mountain carving. Crazy Horse Memorial has been a work in progress since 1947, when Henry Standing Bear convinced Korczak Ziolkowski to carve a sculpture in Thunderhead Mountain to memorialize one of the Lakota's most revered chiefs. Originally Standing Bear wanted Crazy Horse's likeness included on Mount Rushmore, and he repeatedly reached out to Gutzon Borglum. When he received no response, he talked to Korczak, who had worked with Borglum.

I don't know what he said to the guy, but it sure was effective. The Polish-American dedicated his life to the project; his wife, Ruth, dedicated her life to the project; and four of their ten children have dedicated their lives to the project.

What originally was going to be just a mountain carving - although a massive one at that - has become an entire complex dedicated to preserving not only the legacy of Crazy Horse, but also Native American culture. After Korczak's death in 1982, Ruth switched the focus from sculpting the horse to sculpting the face, and she unveiled it seventeen years later. At that point, the project had been in the works for fifty years, and when we visited another twenty years later, it wasn't anywhere close to completion.

What's taking so long?

The answer was inside. We followed the long drive, Crazy Horse's profile in the distance, and paid our $24 entrance fee ($12 each). From the

Crazy Horse Memorial

parking lot, the statue was still far, far away, and we realized we weren't getting any closer unless we paid extra for the bus tour. We opted to just see what we could see and entered the Welcome Center, which housed the gift shop and the Indian Museum of North America. We walked through the gift shop to the courtyard, and we stepped back outside in time to see a man and woman performing traditional dances. Passing a fountain and an alabaster-white model representing Korczak's final vision, we stepped into the Original Lobby and got a picture of the scope of this dream, and the challenges they've been facing to reach it.

From the beginning, the Crazy Horse Memorial has been entirely privately funded. Every entrance fee and every purchase in the gift shop goes towards funding this vision, and they've turned down federal money to remain independent. In addition to the funding issue, there's been opposition from some Native Americans who think carving the likeness of a man who eschewed photographs into a mountain goes against everything Crazy Horse believed.

Despite the obstacles, they continue, and you can't fault the Ziolkowskis' dedication. Ruth, who passed away in 2014, and Korczak are both buried in a tomb the sculptor carved into the mountain, and their children carry on their dream of honoring Native American peoples. In

addition to the museum, the Indian University of North America they founded enables students to complete a summer semester of study at the memorial, and by 2018 the foundation had awarded over $2 million in scholarships to American Indian students.

We browsed Korczak's studio and home and the museum before leaving. After the looking-up-Washington's-nose experience at Mount Rushmore, I suppose I expected we'd be able to get a bit closer, but this was a work in progress, and it's likely to be unfinished for many years to come. When it's complete, it will be a testament to one family's persistence and passion.

The Cheyenne and the Sioux consider the Black Hills the spiritual center of the world, so it seemed fitting that our next stop was the geographical center of the nation that grew up around it.

Except it wasn't; not really.

In Belle Fourche (pronounced *foosh*), South Dakota, there's a monument marking the geographical center of the United States. The center used to be in Kansas, but then Hawaii entered the picture and it shifted. The monument is located at the Center of the Nation Tri-State Museum/Visitor Center. We parked in front of a post marking the Great Western Cattle Trail, which was next to an historical marker explaining this location as the geo-center of the country (sort of). A few yards away were Vietnam and Korean War Memorials, plus an 1876 log cabin, plus another dedication to soldiers who served in the World Wars and the Korean Conflict. There was also a tribute to George Freeman Mortimer, "Friend

of all South Dakota." We were so overwhelmed by the sheer number of monuments we completely missed the *actual* Geographic Center of the Nation Monument located behind the museum, which I guess is OK, since it wasn't the actual center, anyway. The *real* center of the country is about twenty miles away, but it's on private land so the city dedicated a symbolic monument.

We left the close-enough center of the country, drove west, and SD-34 turned into WY-24. If it hadn't been for the billboard that said "WYOMING," which was partially blocked by a parked SUV and a couple of ladies stretching their legs, we'd never have known we'd just entered our fifth state. The thing about driving from one state to another is that you realize there's no discernible difference when you're crossing a border. The topography changes gradually - for the most part, unless you cross a mighty big river, and even that isn't always enough. Sometimes you can tell you're in a different state because the road surface or the speed limit changes, but if your focus is entirely on the landscape, that invisible line never registers.

We passed a town called Aladdin, which seemed to consist solely of an ancient general store with warped wood red siding and animal racks perched above the three second-story windows. A green sign in between one silver and one red mechanical gas pump declared the town had a

Aladdin, Wyoming, Population 15

population of 15 at an elevation of 3740. More signs advertised antiques, which makes sense, since the store had been around since 1896. There was also a bar and a post office, and a clothes rack on the porch offered collared shirts for sale.

A few miles further we drove through Alva, population 50, elevation 3995. I could feel that we were getting closer, and then we crested a hill and caught our first sight of Devils Tower.

Being a child of the '70s, I have seen *Close Encounters of the Third Kind*, which means that my first glimpse of Devils Tower was not a complete shock to my system. But I still wasn't prepared for its impact. Next to the Belle Fourche River, it shoots straight up into the sky. As we neared I could begin to see the vertical lines on its surface, lines that looked like a creature had dragged its claws from summit to base.

We circled the laccolith (*told you you'd see that word again*) and found a campsite under the cottonwoods. We nearly had our pick, so we chose one with a view of the tower. Who am I kidding - in that campground, *every* site had a view of the tower. I was about to get on my bike and ride to the entrance so I could deposit our fee when a park ranger, a large man with a white scruffy beard and two dachshunds sitting next to him, pulled up in his golf cart and offered me a ride. This was Bob from Texas, who volunteered up North during the summers and went home in the winter. We circled the loop and he stopped at each occupied site, making notes in his legal pad about who was leaving when while his dogs licked my face. After I dropped my envelope at the pay station, he kindly returned me to Jim and wished us luck on our journey.

That night I breaded pork chops and paired them with a salad of iceberg, cherry tomatoes, cheese, and ranch dressing. It felt like a Western-y type meal to make on our first night in Wyoming. After dinner we sauntered over to the amphitheater for the evening program, which had already started. When we sat down, the ranger, a petite and passionate Native American woman, was explaining that more than twenty tribes consider Devils Tower a sacred monument. The name is wrong, she explained. The nations that consider it sacred call it Bear's Lodge, Home of the Bear, Aloft on a Rock, Tree Rock, Great Gray Horn, Brown Buffalo Horn - none of which mean "devil." Yet when Army Commander Richard Irving Dodge visited in 1875 on a scientific expedition, he wrote that the Indians called it Bad God Tower, which he changed to Devil's Tower. Some think it was just a bad translation; others, like the ranger, think it might have been intentional. "One of the tactics {of conquest} is to take away the place names," she said. There have been several efforts to change the name to Bear Lodge, a translation from the Lakota *Mato Tipila*, but they've been shot down every time.

We walked the short path back to our campsite and quickly put everything away for the evening. A strong wind ripped through the flat lands surrounding the tower and kept up most of the night, but we felt strangely at peace.

DAY 8

The wind whipped my hair as I walked to the Belle Fourche River that morning, the sun's sideways rays turning the landscape into an impressionist painting. I ignored the cheek lashings from my ponytail and felt the magnificence, the sheer splendor of Devils Tower.

It's hard for me to call it that. Everything about that name is wrong. Not only was it a bad translation, but it's also missing an apostrophe. When it was officially declared a National Monument, the possessive punctuation was left out by mistake.

Devils Tower is a clerical error.

You know what wasn't a clerical error? Our marriage license! Good thing, because not only were we starting our second week on this crazy trip, it was also our third anniversary. When we said our vows (Well, I said mine. He *sang* his. Show-off. Remarkable, romantic, stop-you're-ruining-my-makeup-oh-who-cares-keep-singing show-off.), we didn't have month-long road trips in our plans. We had the whole death do us part bit, and the I'll love you forever part, but we didn't know it would also mean that we'd take extended cross-country trips so that I could write books about them. It was a dream of mine, but it wasn't one I thought would *actually* happen.

But it did. And there we were. Standing at the base of the first National Monument in the United States.

On the way out of the campground we stopped at the Circle of Sacred Smoke, a sculpture by Junkyu Muto that symbolizes peace. It represents a puff of smoke as it first leaves the pipe and is meant to raise awareness of the twenty tribes that consider the peak sacred. As someone who has always been sensitive to the near-eradication of Native Americans, that sculpture and the Ranger talk from the night before, combined with other experiences, profoundly moved me. After visiting several National Parks in a relatively short amount of time, a picture was emerging of a rogue branch of the U.S. government that gave a damn about what it did to people.

After Bear Butte, and the Black Hills, and the broken Treaty of Fort Laramie, I was grateful to see a National Monument that not only acknowledged the people who'd lived here for thousands and thousands of years, but also included them as an integral part of the experience.

It wasn't even nine in the morning when we reached the Visitor Center and it was already a happening place. The log building was the definition of rustic. Constructed of ponderosa pines in 1935 by the Civilian Conservation Corps, it's on the National Register of Historic Places and was exactly what you'd expect a National Park Visitor Center to be. Inside, we browsed the exhibits covering the monument's human and geologic history, and eavesdropped as a Junior Ranger raised her right hand to accept her newly-sworn duties. Outside, people gathered for a guided walk around the behemoth. We took off in the opposite direction.

The Tower Path is an easy 1.3 mile hike that encircles Devils Tower. It winds through a pine forest around the ever-present massive monolith. Here and there we'd come across strips of cloth and bundles tied to tree branches. Native peoples leave these physical manifestations of prayers around the base of this sacred place, and they are not to be disturbed. Seeing them is to experience an intimacy with another person's faith, like an offering at a memorial or a lit candle on an altar.

As we walked I felt gratitude that people in the late 1800s had the foresight to preserve this landmark for the public. In 1890, the General Land

Prayer cloths at Devils Tower

Office (GLO) ordered that all applications for ownership of the tower and the land around it should be rejected. This same organization administered the Homestead Act, which parceled out pieces of land to people who wanted to live on it (except the native peoples who were already there). In 1892, the GLO (precursor to the Bureau of Land Management, or BLM) protected the landmark further by making it a temporary forest reserve. It held that designation until 1906, when President Theodore Roosevelt used his wiles to have Devils Tower declared the first National Monument.

I kinda feel like Teddy pulled a fast one. He'd originally signed the act to prevent looting of Native American ruins and artifacts, a practice that had become an issue in Chaco Canyon and similar archaeological sites in the southwest. The Antiquities Act, signed on June 8, 1906, gave President Roosevelt, and all subsequent presidents, the power to declare "historic landmarks, historic and prehistoric structures, and other objects of historic or scientific interest" as monuments. While Devils Tower technically fit those criteria, considering the reason for the act it's a little surprising that the Wyoming site was chosen as the first officially protected landmark. Hey, whatever works. I'm just glad he did.

Up close, Devils Tower is even more astonishing. It's made up of columns that are unexpectedly symmetrical. Huge chunks lay around the base and when we looked up, we could see where they broke off. On the northeast side, peregrine falcons swirled around their nests. A little further and we joined a group of hikers pointing binoculars and zoom lenses at a sole climber.

Normally there'd be more than one person scaling the columns. Devils Tower is a climbing destination, and has been since 1893 when William Rogers and Willard Ripley used a wooden stake ladder to get to the summit, a relatively flat plain the size of a football field. Two years later, William's wife Linnie became the first woman to reach the top. Now there are over 200 mapped routes and climbers travel from all over the world to scale Bear Lodge, as it's known to the Lakota.

For those who consider this a sacred place, like the Lakota, it's been said that each stake is felt physically and psychologically, and climbing is akin to climbing a cross. Each tribe has a different story, but a frequently seen element is that a bear attempted to reach the summit and kept slipping, dragging its claws in the rock. On the way down, it left those distinctive vertical scores that make climbing it so enticing. As Bear Lodge became increasingly popular with climbers, the Park Service realized it needed to acknowledge the importance of this place to the many tribes who consider it sacred. At first they tried a voluntary halt to climbing in June, with a mandatory shutdown for commercial guides, but they lost a lawsuit initiated by the Mountain States Legal Foundation. So, in 1995 they established a completely voluntary ban for individuals and guides during that same month.

Most people honor it. Obviously, as we watched a man hunt for his next hold, some don't.

Catching up with the guided tour that had gone the other way around the mountain, we joined them briefly as the Ranger talked about prescribed burns. We'd noticed there was very little undergrowth in the forest, and that's because the Park Service intentionally starts fires.

Smokey Bear would not be upset by this. During our hike we'd seen discolored bark at the base of several trees. Turns out, ponderosa pines are built for flames. Not only does it take an incredibly hot fire to burn through their thick bark, their sap is also a fire suppressant. As a fire gets taller, the lower branches act like a natural sprinkler system.

How cool is that?

It only works if there are regular fires, however. From 1916 until the 1970s the Park Service actively suppressed fires, building up decades of kindling. Since 1991, Devils Tower has regularly burned sections of the surrounding forest floor in spring and fall, mimicking the natural cycle. If you happen to visit and see portions of the park on fire, don't be alarmed. It's probably on purpose.

Surprisingly, considering everything we'd seen and learned that morning, it was only 11 o'clock when we resumed our westward journey. By 12:14pm we'd caught our first glimpse of snow-capped mountains. Yep, I noted the time. I see white summits and squeal like 15-year-old me if she'd met Mikhail Baryshnikov. (*White Nights*, anyone?) No wonder I married a Mountain Man.

We picked up I-90, drove through the mining town of Gillette, and curved north towards Montana. I'd mentioned earlier that we'd be taking a convoluted route; this was part of it. We were driving from Wyoming into Montana to drive back into Wyoming. We had a good reason for it. I swear.

Knowing we'd be driving this route, Paul, our cattle-ranching host in South Dakota, had suggested one more stop. We pulled off in Sheridan to see King's Saddlery and King Ropes & Museum.

You know how somebody mentions a place and you're like "Yeah yeah yeah ok. I'll go, just because you want me to go." And then you go, not expecting much, and walk in and think "Holy Mother of Leather-working!

What magic is this place!" And it's stuffed to the rafters with rows and rows of saddles tooled with the most intricate designs you could ever imagine burned into leather, coupled with an unreasonable number of spurs, stirrups, tools, mounted heads, skulls, guns, and whips, plus a stagecoach, a one-horse open sleigh, a stuffed bear, and a bull's head wearing goggles?

It was like that.

King's Saddlery

If you know saddles, then you know King's Saddlery. Don King, who passed away in 2007, began his saddle business in 1946 and became recognized for his floral pattern, known as the Sheridan style. In the sixties he added rope-making, and the family-owned business still makes them by hand. We walked into the store and knew this wasn't for tourists. "Real cowboys shop here," I thought. Out back we found the museum, a sprawling collection of just about every Western item you could imagine. We marveled at the scope and on the way out we talked with Bill, Don's son, for a bit.

"We all collected something," he said of his dad, his three brothers, and "even my wife." At first they had a Quonset hut of old carriages, but things kept piling up, so they turned it into a museum.

We walked out a little shell-shocked, recovering by stopping at each of several bronze sculptures that lined the sidewalk. Across the street a neon cowboy rode a bucking bronco at The Mint Bar, est. 1907.

Note to self: don't go to Sheridan, Wyoming, if all you have is two hours. In the short time we were there it had fulfilled just about every expectation I'd had of a rustling western town, and I was sad to leave it. We didn't have a choice, though. The next day we had a date with Yellowstone.

"Woohoo! We're in Montana!"

Our eighth state. I knew we wouldn't be here long, but this was Jim's home state and that deserved a little celebration. Unfortunately, the joviality was short-lived. Our next stop was a place where hundreds of men died.

We make a habit of visiting places like that. Battlefields, internment camps, memorials. It's not because we're morbid. Just the opposite. We visit because it's important to learn from the past, and the only way you can do that is to see it all, the good, the bad, and the devastating.

Little Bighorn Battlefield National Monument is proof that perception of the past morphs when seen through a changing societal lens. This was a memorial to people who fought and died in a battle that took place in 1876, so you might think something that happened so long ago would be static. Yet, before 1991 it was known as Custer Battlefield National Monument and focused solely on Army casualties.

The battle that took place was part of the Great Sioux War and

Monuments for fallen Sioux

could be traced back to the broken Treaty of Fort Laramie. It was nineteen years after Sitting Bull and Crazy Horse had met with other leaders at Bear Butte in 1857 to discuss the threat the settlers presented, and eight years after gold-rushing settlers trod on the infamous treaty and stole the Black Hills. By the time Lt. Gen. George Armstrong Custer and the 7th Cavalry arrived at the Little Bighorn River on June 25, 1876, thousands of Lakota, Northern Cheyenne, and Arapaho were camped along its banks. The battle was disastrous for the U.S., who suffered 268 casualties, including Custer. The tribes lost anywhere from 40 to 100 warriors.

This was the site of Custer's Last Stand, but it was more than that. It was one of the final battles in a war between two cultures that were inherently unable to coexist. One, a nomadic people who followed the land and went where the living was best. The other, a people who settled a land and made it what they wanted.

Prior to 1991, only the U.S. story was told at the battlefield. After a 1988 protest by members of the American Indian Movement and combined pressure from that group and the National Congress for American Indians, Congress passed legislation requiring both sides of the story be told. On December 10, 1991, President George H. W. Bush signed it into law and the site became Little Bighorn Battlefield National Monument. In addition to the name change, there is also an Indian Memorial with engraved granite walls and a bronze sculpture of Native American Spirit Warriors.

Visiting is somber. There are gravestones marking spots where soldiers and warriors fell. There's a horse cemetery. Most somber of all is the memorial etched with names above a mass grave of about 220 soldiers, scouts, and civilians. There are several headstones inside the fence near the memorial, and there is even one for Custer, although his remains were moved to West Point. (His horse, Comanche, survived the battle and ended up at Fort Meade.)

We began to walk the path next to the graveyard when I heard, for the second time in my life, a rattlesnake in the wild.

This wasn't like my rattlesnake encounter in the Badlands. There were no juicy tourists to entice the snake away from me. Here, it was just the two of us, separated by a wrought iron fence. I told him to stay on his side and I'd stay on mine, but we both knew that line was an illusion. I slowly backed away, and Jim and I decided it was time to go.

DAY 9

We'd chosen to overnight in an Extended Stay in Billings and, well rested, I practically jumped out of bed. Today was Yellowstone Day! And, AND, not only was it Yellowstone Day, it was Beartooth Highway Day!

I was a wee bit excited.

After a few days of emotional, information-packed experiences, we were ready for a pretty drive and a couple of nights in the first National Park. It was the beginning of June, and Beartooth Highway cut through the snow-capped peaks I'd been ogling the day before. From year to year, there's no telling when this scenic drive will be open. We'd lucked out. This year, the plows cleared the final stretch on May 18, a little less than three weeks before our excursion.

Our route to Yellowstone was US-212, and although we could have taken it all the way from Belle Fourche, we would have missed Devils Tower, Sheridan, and Little Bighorn. While those destinations exacerbated our convoluted, roundabout route, they were worth the extra miles.

The road from Billings to Red Lodge was a fairly straight course through a flat plain. It looked like it was going to dead-end at a big wall of a mountain in our windshield. Through the town, 212 was lined with two-story buildings flying U.S. and Montana flags. We passed a Carnegie library, a theater marquee advertising handmade chocolates, and a church that looked like a rook. A wayside exhibit near the end of town informed us that the Beartooth Plateau was made up of the oldest exposed rocks in Montana and some of the oldest on Earth.

Five minutes out of town the road curved, and curved again, following the swerves of what was now a valley. We climbed higher. Deciduous trees gave way to evergreens. A creek (crick? spring?) gurgled and cascaded. We pulled over to listen to it for a bit, then hopped back in and continued ascending higher and higher until we reached the open gates telling us that Beartooth Highway was open for business. Charles Kuralt considered this stretch of road "the most beautiful drive in America," and we were about to see for ourselves.

It was a partly cloudy day, and the landscape was random splotches

of gray and green with streaks of snowy white. As we got higher, the valley got greener and the shoulders got steeper. More rocks, less grass. We followed the switchbacks up up up and could see where we'd be, eventually. We pulled over and jumped in the snow, startled when a man wearing ski boots came out of the woods. Driving higher and higher, there were large swaths with no growth at all, and I imagined an avalanche clearing everything in its path. The higher we drove, the shorter the trees. Maybe they just seemed shorter, because everything else was beyond a measurable scale. Melting runoff trickled here and there, feeding the creek we'd left some time ago. It was nearly all brown now. Just a few trees holding things in their place. The blacktop, considering its annual freeze and thaw, was in excellent condition and I wondered how often they repaved it.

At 9,190 feet we pulled off at Rock Creek Vista Point. We walked to the overlook and chipmunks scampered. (That's what they do, right? They scamper?) A raven flew and we looked over the tops of peaks and down down down into the valley below.

The view from Rock Creek Vista Point on the Beartooth Highway

In the distance the clouds grew darker, so we left the vista and continued towards Yellowstone. And climbed up. And up. And up. Being the passenger, my view was a whole lot of air. There was a guardrail, at least, but I wasn't sure how much protection it would provide. Thank goodness there wasn't much traffic and Jim is an excellent driver.

Soon the trees were gone and we were in the clouds, driving between ever-deeper snow banks. Stakes lined the shoulder to indicate where the road was supposed to be when the snow covered the pavement completely. We entered Wyoming again. We drove through a passage where the stakes were completely buried and after a few more turns came across people skiing. Ah - that's where that guy had come from.

The darker clouds were no longer in the distance. They were coming in fast, and lightning peppered their approach. We began descending through rain and sleet. Finally we drove into patches of blue and the storm stayed behind like a petulant child.

With the squall safely behind us, we pulled off at Beartooth Lake. It was simply breathtaking. Pines stood on half of the opposite shore, and a bare slope and butte rose out of the other, both reflected in the alpine water.

Beartooth Lake

Just past the lake we crossed a tall bridge and noticed a waterfall. We pulled to the side of the road in front of a few other cars and walked back. This was unlike any waterfall I'd ever seen, or heard, or experienced. The sheer power overwhelmed the senses. I couldn't fathom the volume of water pummeling through the canyon lined with pines, and the noise drowned out every other sound. The current was entirely froth and, despite the onslaught, a tiny tree growing out of a rock in the center held fast. We hadn't even gotten to Yellowstone yet, and I could barely speak.

Beartooth Highway turned north back into Montana, cut through Cooke City, and 68 miles from those open gates it ended and Yellowstone National Park began. The Northeast Entrance station, like the visitor center in Devils Tower, was also constructed in 1935 and with the same rustic style. The ranger gave us our map and our Visitor Guide and pointed us in the direction of Madison Campground. I had reserved our spot back in April, somehow securing the last reservable campsite for the dates we wanted to be there.

We were soon back in Wyoming, and we'd be in that state for three nights. We wouldn't see Montana again until we were headed back east, and then Jim would show me his childhood.

One of the tenets of fiction is creating a suspension of disbelief. The author's goal is to construct a world that's so real that the reader forgets it isn't.

Mother Nature needs to work on that.

The deeper we ventured into the park, the more vivid the colors became. We were soon drenched in emerald grass and pastel blue skies and more of those bright white cotton ball clouds that seemed to show up with regularity on this journey. A herd of bison rambled and lollygagged along the side of the road. We pulled off by a wide, meandering creek studded with sandbars and smelled a hint of sulfur. This was the Lamar Valley and we were getting closer to the caldera, the hotbed of geothermal activity.

We stopped at Tower Falls because we knew we wouldn't get back that way again. Then we drove through groves of bare lodgepole pines, remnants of a past fire surrounded by new growth.

And then, steam billowed from the earth and we were in the dragon's lair.

Growing up in Missoula, Montana, Jim had been to Yellowstone before. He'd seen the hot breath of the burning center of the earth. For him, it was the stuff of experiences remembered and the excitement of seeing them again. For me, it was a whole new mythical, unbelievable, world.

We reached the campground a little after seven. Our sprawling site

Tower Falls, Yellowstone National Park

Lamar Valley, Yellowstone National Park

backed against the woods. Fellow campers included families, a couple of guys who slept in hammocks strung high enough that the bears couldn't reach them, an adventure guide leading a tour, and a group of students from Teton Science Schools.

This was bear country, which meant that just about anything we weren't wearing, sleeping on, or sleeping in, had to be secured inside Jeannie the Jeep. The idea of setting up our camp kitchen just to break it down and store it again was more than we could bear, so we settled for cold bagels and went to bed.

Tomorrow was going to be a beautiful day.

Steam rising from the earth

DAY 10

People often ask me what part of this road trip was my favorite. What was my favorite park, where was my favorite destination, what was my favorite experience.

To use a cliché, that's like choosing a favorite child.

BUT.

But, this day was up there.

It was the place, yes, because you cannot *not* be moved by Yellowstone, but more than that it was a singular moment of kindness. It will forever stand out, especially whenever things are bleak or when I doubt humanity's capacity for compassion.

Traffic started early that morning. I could hear cars at 6:30, and while it initially surprised me, I realized it shouldn't. The park is nearly 3,500 square miles. Most of that may be wilderness, but it still takes a lot of people to manage the millions that visit every year. It was chilly when I stepped out of the tent and I was glad I had a stash of knit caps and had put on four layers before going to bed. (What? I get cold.) We shared our last breakfast bar. It was a fast meal; we needed to get moving before the masses hit.

If I can give you one tip for visiting Yellowstone National Park, it is this: get up early and go to Old Faithful first. Don't cook breakfast, don't stop along the way, don't dilly-dally. Just go.

Even with our abbreviated morning routine, it still took us an hour to get out of Madison campground. We were on the road by 7:30, and ignoring every desire to pull over save one, made it to Old Faithful within 40 minutes. Along the way we drove through steam so thick in places it looked like the ground was on fire. By 8:10am it was already getting crowded. Inside the visitor center we checked the time of the next eruption, and since it was projected to happen in just a few minutes we made our way outside to the benches. There were two rows that wrapped around a portion of the geyser. The first was full, so we stood on top of the back row.

As we waited we could see steam rising from the earth in multiple places, stretching out in a row towards the tree line. The crowd was quiet. Eventually, the steam from Old Faithful billowed higher and higher, and

although we couldn't see much of the eruption, we could hear the water sizzle as it landed on the scorched earth. I expected a bombastic explosion, but it seemed calm and kind of gradual, probably because it was hidden by the steam. Still, it was something to behold and imagining the pressure required to push that stream of boiling water more than 100 feet in the air, pressure that had been building under our feet, was humbling.

Bicycles were allowed on the route from Old Faithful to Morning Glory, a short path that's only two miles round-trip. We helmeted up and rode, stopping at each hydrothermal feature in turn. Next to Castle Geyser a bubbling pool rimmed with crusted white minerals and orange mud intermittently boiled, and then steam would roll out of the neighboring cone like a puffing train engine. Across the path Shield Spring simmered, and further down Grotto Geyser looked for all the world as if a mythical beast had collapsed and turned to stone, eroding over the centuries.

At the end of the trail, Morning Glory hot spring was a rainbow of orange, yellow, green, and blue surrounded by a ring of white. At the edges, dead lodgepole pines wore "bobby socks" and reminded me of Iowa's White Pole Road. The trees had wicked up the mineral-rich water, and after the moisture evaporated a ring of silica stayed behind.

We quickly rode back to Jeannie and munched on trail mix while

Grotto Geyser

we drove to Biscuit Basin. We parked and a sign warned us that the area was volatile and unpredictable. Another pointed out that the ground was so acidic in some spots that it could burn through boots, so stay on the boardwalk and don't be an idiot. Streams of steaming rivulets flowed into the Firehole River. Pools of bright aqua looked painted, and amazingly, confoundingly, wildflowers popped up near bleached and contorted trees.

Hordes of tourists from a pair of buses blocked sections of the boardwalk and we carefully, very carefully, sidled by so we wouldn't get dumped into the scalding, burning earth by a stray selfie-stick. It was our first encounter with the masses and we decided that any future stops would be dictated by the number of tour buses in the parking lot.

The hike up to Grand Prismatic Spring Overlook was just six-tenths of a mile from the trailhead with an elevation gain of 105 feet. It only took us ten minutes, even with a flatlander (me) leading the way. Fortunately, I had trained before we left so I'd be in better shape, because even though that trail was short, when it began at an elevation of 7,270 feet with some fairly steep spots, it wasn't necessarily easy.

At the base of the trail, where it split off from the Fairy Falls hike, we stopped to stare at the steam floating above the hot spring. It was, and I kid you not, orange and blue. We made our way up and caught glimpses through the trees. After one tight turn and final steep stretch, we stepped

onto the platform and looked at the largest hot spring in the United States, and the third largest in the world.

Grand Prismatic Spring is aptly named, and it was easy to see why early reports of Yellowstone's natural wonders were dismissed as the ravings of crazed lunatics. But after enough stories, skeptics could no longer deny that these fantastical descriptions may be real.

Grand Prismatic Spring

We picked our way down the trail. About halfway through our descent we stepped to the side to allow a trio to pass. It was a man and woman carrying another man in a running wheelchair. They set him down for a moment and she leaned in to check on him, and then they picked him up again and resumed their hike.

This. This was one of the kindest gestures, one of the most humble displays of humanity I have ever seen. It's a moment I grasp and clutch, this privilege of witnessing these selfless people. I made up stories in my mind, but they all had the same moral: two people went to extraordinary lengths to make sure another could see a magnificent view.

Our next stop was going to be the spring itself, but after seeing three tour buses in the packed parking lot, we decided we'd come back early the next morning on our way out. We drove north and I nearly broke out in hives. Traffic heading the other direction towards Old Faithful was backed up for miles. MILES. I wanted to tell them "turn around, see something else, don't sit in traffic in YELLOWSTONE." We took a detour on Firehole Lake Drive and found a secluded picnic spot nestled in the pines. An unexpected benefit of being in bear country was that we had to keep our kitchen with us, and we fired up the Coleman and heated up burgers I'd cooked in the Extended Stay in Billings. While we ate, just the two of us in a sunny spot on a hill, I thought of all those people we had passed and hoped they found a quiet place of their own.

The day was disappearing quickly. We packed out what we'd packed in and drove on, wanting to see everything we possibly could in our short time at this amazing place.

Norris Geyser Basin sits at an intersection of three fault lines. It is the hottest, oldest, and the most volatile of all of Yellowstone's hot spots. On one side is Back Basin, known for trees and Steamboat Geyser, the

Porcelain Basin

tallest geyser in the world. On the other, Porcelain Basin, a white-washed depression spotted with color. In the middle is the Norris Geyser Basin Museum, an original trail museum built in 1929 - 1930.

We walked through the breezeway and entered the museum, browsing the displays and learning that those various colors we'd seen around the hot springs were actually itty-bitty tiny creatures. The green was heat-loving algae and the red and orange were thermophiles and "extremophiles," a real term for microorganisms that survive in extreme environments.

Stray hat in a pool of thermophiles

By this time it was mid-afternoon, so we walked the Porcelain Basin route because it was shorter. Plus, the park was doing construction on the boardwalk in Back Basin. With thermal features at least 199°F, which is boiling point at that elevation, it's surprising there was a boardwalk at all. We took the steep walk down past fumaroles, quite literally openings in the earth's crust that spew sulphuric steam, towards an almost-blinding valley. No wildflowers sprouted there and it was nearly devoid of trees. A bronze hat made of straw sat in a steaming pool the same shade and I clamped onto my cap to make sure it didn't suffer a similar fate.

We'd hiked. We'd biked. We'd narrowly avoided being dumped into ground that could dissolve our very bones. My feet throbbed. My body ached. But this was Yellowstone! So, we kept going.

A quick stop at the National Park Ranger Museum was non-negotiable. Park Rangers are some of my favorite people. I'm normally loathe to lump any group, but every person I've met that works in a National Park has been helpful, enthusiastic, and passionate. Bruce and Collins, retired rangers at the museum, were no exception. Collins had to be in her 70s, yet she told us how she'd backpacked in Grand Teton that past weekend.

I want to be her when I grow up.

It was after 4pm, so we asked the two volunteers whether we should go to Mammoth Hot Springs or the Grand Canyon of the Yellowstone.

"Canyon, no question," urged Bruce. So to the canyon we went.

This canyon, this Grand Canyon of the Yellowstone, did not seem real. It was a painting of a canyon. It was a pastel gash. Spiny slopes of yellow, coral, and rust led my eye to a narrow river of rapids. It wasn't just rust-colored. It was actual rust created when the iron in the rhyolite was exposed to moisture and oxygen. We turned to look the other direction; the waterfall that fed those rapids cut through the pines and dropped in a wide band. We wanted to climb down the trail and get closer, but that would've meant we had to climb back up. It was getting late, we were getting hungry, and we still wanted to see the other side of the canyon. So, we drove and parked again, and got close enough to the falls to feel the spray and touch the rainbow, and we kissed and I said "yes."

Eleven hours after leaving camp we returned. I made up for our bagel the night before with a dinner of shrimp cocktail followed by ditali topped with Italian tomatoes, ground beef, and mushrooms. It had been an amazing day. An exciting, exhausting, awe-inspiring, humbling, and amazing day.

Grand Canyon of the Yellowstone River

DAY 11

In 1872, during an era of unprecedented growth and the continued doctrine of Manifest Destiny, the U.S. government decided to set aside nearly 3,500 square miles for the enjoyment of its people. That land couldn't be bought, stolen, or borrowed. It was there for everyone, and was a remarkable development at a time of almost rabid desire for expansion and ownership.

It happened because not everyone thought Manifest Destiny, the idea that the U.S. had a divine right to take over whatever land it wanted, was a great idea. I learned in school that the policy of expansion was *the* policy. I never learned that there was opposition or that a vast number of citizens and politicians thought it was not only poppycock, but also immoral, amoral, and oppressive.

Fortunately, President Ulysses S. Grant was one of those politicians who thought land-grabbing wasn't always a good thing. He turned that belief into law by signing legislation that created our first National Park. Ulysses S. Grant gave us Yellowstone.

We were up and out by 8:30 so we could get to Grand Prismatic Spring before the throngs, making a quick stop to take a photo of an actual, real live working phone booth near the campground entrance. (There's little to no cell service in Yellowstone, and that's how you can call if there's an emergency. It's quite anachronistic.) We got to the spring and found a parking spot just as a couple of tour buses were unloading, so we raced to the boardwalk and crossed over the Firehole River. On the way, Excelsior Geyser exhaled so much steam that we only knew it was there because a sign told us. A thick crowd milled near the spring itself. It was a polite group, with people shuffling in and out so everyone could see and get the obligatory photos. I overheard a retired man and woman talking about the National Parks they've visited.

"I never made it to Denali," she said.

"You didn't miss anything," he countered.

WHAT?

I had to step away from that nonsense, and we went the opposite direction of the tour bus denizens, who were selfie-by-selfie getting closer to the main attraction. By the time we got back to the river, we'd counted five hats that had been blown into the unrecoverable muck. We walked over the bridge as runoff from Excelsior dumped 4,000 gallons of boiling water into the river and we grumbled about the people beyond the "KEEP OUT - Revegetation Area" sign on the other side. Showing remarkable restraint, I did not point at them and scream "They're degrading the surface!"

But I wanted to. Oh, boy, I wanted to.

We crossed the Continental Divide, twice, before stopping at West Thumb Geyser Basin. I thought we might be done with the geothermal portion of the visit, but nope. Instead, we entered a caldera within a caldera, one as large as Crater Lake in Oregon.

About 600,000 years ago, an enormous volcano erupted leaving behind Yellowstone Caldera, a 30- by 45-mile basin. It was the third in a series of super-eruptions, the first of which had happened two million years ago, give or take a few millennia. Then 174,000 years ago another volcano in the same vicinity erupted, leaving behind what is now the West Thumb of Yellowstone Lake.

West Thumb of Yellowstone Lake

A boardwalk surrounded the geyser basin, part of it bordering the shore of the lake. It was an odd juxtaposition in a land of odd juxtapositions. On one side, a calm lake with mild ripples. On the other, a steaming chasm rimmed by green grass and yellow flowers, followed by ground leached of color surrounding an even deeper, bluer pool. Here and there were puddles of orange. In a sun-drenched glen of pines, an elk with a matted mane ate, ignoring the shutter clicks just a few yards away.

We made one more stop at one more waterfall, and then our Yellowstone visit was over.

One last Yellowstone waterfall

The South Entrance of Yellowstone National Park leads to the North Entrance of Grand Teton National Park. The two are connected by the John D. Rockefeller, Jr. Memorial Parkway. We'd been on it since West Thumb, and would be for the next 27 miles. I was a bit surprised to see a parkway named after the financier and philanthropist. As I found out later, he deserved it.

It was Day 11, and the constant *everything* caught up with me. Sore throat, pressure headache, congestion. It felt like a cold, but we thought it might be altitude sickness combined with the sunburn I'd picked up. Whatever it was, it sucked.

I temporarily forgot about my discomfort when we stopped at Jackson Lake Overlook.

It was pristine. Sky-blue lake in front of us, raggedy peaks streaked with snow in the distance, tall grass and random wildflowers at our feet.

Surreal. Unreal. Pristine.

When you're standing in that majesty, it doesn't matter how you feel. It's a place that consumes thought and screams LOOK AT ME.

We didn't have a campsite reserved, so we stopped at the Colter Bay Visitor Center complex. I asked Joanie, the first ranger we found, what would be the best way to explore Grand Teton in my less-than-optimal state. She told me to drink lots of water (check), eat something salty (check), and drive to Gros Ventre campground. Joanie had been a ranger at Grand Teton for twenty years, so when she said that campground rarely filled, even though it was Saturday, we believed her. Figuring we had a little time to spare, we got a slice of pizza at the cafe and took advantage of their wifi to check email before driving south.

Sometimes on this road trip we'd listen to the radio. Mostly music from the 70s and 80s. Often, however, we drove in silence. We weren't mad or upset, and it wasn't that we had nothing to say to each other. It was simply that what we were witnessing through the windshield said it for us.

The Grand Tetons were like nothing I'd ever seen. They're like nothing most people have ever seen, considering they're made up of some of the oldest rock on earth. The range is the definition of "jagged peaks." That may be a trope, a lazy description, except there's little else that so aptly describes these mountains. While the rocks themselves are ancient, their upthrust from the earth is recent, relatively speaking. Age and erosion haven't had a chance to smooth out their rough edges, so there they stand. Jagged.

We followed the Snake River south. Knowing there was construction at the turn to our campground, we avoided it with a quick stop at Mormon Row Historic District. Turning the corner from Antelope Flats Road, I instantly recognized the barn. It's an iconic image of the west, with its peaked roof and the mountain range in the background. It's been said the T.A. Moulton Barn is the most photographed barn in America. I added to that statistic, and we continued south.

Gros Ventre (pronounced *grow vaunt*) Campground borders the river of the same name. It's in the middle of a grove of cottonwood trees, and with more than 300 sites is one of the bigger campgrounds in which we stayed. Although there are a few electric spots and room for RVs, they've also got a tent-only loop. Since that meant no generators kicking on early in the morning, we took one of those sites and quickly set up before heading

Grand Tetons

back out to the park. I still didn't feel great, but I wasn't about to curl up on the air mattress. I told my body to chill out and stop being a brat. We had no time for these shenanigans.

Our next stop was the scene of another iconic photograph. The Snake River Overlook is the place where legendary landscape photographer Ansel Adams took one of his most famous photos. Hired by the National Park Service, in 1942 Adams stood on top of a Pontiac and captured a shot that helped save Jackson Hole Valley.

At the time, Grand Teton National Park was a third of its current self, a mere 96,000 acres compared to today's 310,000. The valley that Adams captured wasn't part of that park. In fact, it was a hotbed of controversy. Starting in the late 1920s, John D. Rockefeller, Jr. had been buying up land through a shell enterprise known as the Snake River Valley Company with the intention of giving the goods to the National Park Service. His agents told the sellers that it would be used for conservation purposes, but they didn't know *what* conservation purposes. When the sellers found out who was buying it, and why, they were livid. (For one, they could have gotten Rockefeller prices instead of just plain ol' fair market value.)

Snake River

Congress, led by the Wyoming delegation, kept refusing to take the land. By 1942, Rockefeller was done and threatened to sell to the highest bidder if the government didn't want it. After all, he'd spent $1.5 million to gather it up, and he was trying to *give* it to them. Surprisingly, even though this land was meant for the people, public sentiment was against the idea - until Ansel Adams' photo showed them what they'd be missing. Since Wyoming was still vehemently opposed, President Franklin Delano Roosevelt used his fifth cousin Theodore Roosevelt's Antiquities Act to create the Jackson Hole National Monument. In 1950, it was combined with the National Park. To recognize Rockefeller's role in preserving this area for all, a 24,000 acre parcel between Yellowstone and Grand Teton was established in 1972 and named the John D. Rockefeller, Jr. Memorial Parkway.

After a stop at the Jackson Lake dam, we returned to camp. I sniffled my way through a dinner of chipotle chicken (pre-seasoned) and baked beans (canned) and willed my body to get over itself.

DAY 12

"I want to meet the person who can fold tarps," Jim grumbled. "They must have mad ninja folding skills. Fitted sheet level." So began Day 12.

I couldn't blame him. A) Tarps are notoriously uncooperative. B) It was the eighth time, in twelve days, he had to fold the darn things.

By this time, I knew I didn't have altitude sickness. It was a plain, common, blasted cold. Jim had his tarps; I had my sniffles. They couldn't stop us. We were *going* to enjoy this majestic scenery.

Our first stop was a return to Mormon Row. I wanted a little more time to explore and take a few more pictures. It was a straight line of buildings, a settlement formerly known as Grovont. When the Mormons homesteaded the valley in 1896, they named their new home Gros Ventre after the nearby river, but three years later the U.S. Post Office changed the name because it was too hard to spell.

We explored the buildings north of Antelope Flats first. There was a pink stucco home that seemed distinctly out of place, and a Gambrel barn reminiscent of the Brown Street Inn, the cottage-style mansion we'd stayed in at the start of the trip. An irrigation channel dug by the Mormons still flowed. Back on the south side of the strip, I took my place in front of T.A. Moulton's barn and immediately met a lady with curly auburn hair and a big smile. She was from Connecticut, about my age, and this was her second solo road trip. We took our pictures of the barn and the range behind it and watched a large, vocal raven accompanied by three smaller birds. It was another micro-interaction that public lands enable. If she and I had spent more time together we might have learned that we have more in common than a shared experience, but at that moment, that was all we needed.

The guide and map to Menor's Ferry, available for the price of a dollar, suggested that visitors begin their tour to the left towards the white building. We, of course, went to the right.

It wasn't intentional; it was just the way we decided to go.

This Historic District, designated as such in 1969, was named for entrepreneur and homesteader William D. Menor. He planted his stake in

T.A. Moulton Barn

the ground in 1894, a few years before the Mormons arrived on the other side of the river. But I'll get to him later.

The first building we saw was the Noble Cabin. It had originally been built on Cottonwood Creek, and Maud (or Maude) Noble moved the cabin in 1917 (or 1918) to its spot next to the Snake River. Neither the spelling of Ms. Noble's first name nor when the cabin was moved is clear. The historic plaque on the cabin spelled her name *Maud*, and said the building was erected in 1917. The map and guide called her *Maude*, and said the cabin was moved in 1918.

Either way, it seems that Ms. Noble was an influential woman during a time when women weren't.

In 1923, residents concerned about the increasing development of Jackson Hole met in Maud(e)'s cabin. With more tourism came commercialization and the realization that the valley's popularity could lead to its demise. These conservationists decided that they needed a wealthy patron to start buying up the land and donating it so it could be preserved. (You see where this is going.) One of the attendees was Superintendent of Yellowstone National Park Horace Albright, and a few years later he met none other than John D. Rockefeller, Jr. Practicing what she preached,

Maud(e) sold her land to the Snake River Land Company in 1929.

Our next stop was the Transportation Shed, which housed a covered wagon, a dogsled, a bullboat replica, a plow, and one of the original yellow wagons that toured Yellowstone. We then followed the swiftly-flowing Snake River and stopped at the ferry crossing, a contraption consisting of a floating platform and a cable system that pulled the raft across.

We ended where we were supposed to begin, at William (Bill) D. Menor's whitewashed cabin and general store.

It takes a special sort of character to survive, alone, in a hostile environment, and create a living from scratch. I was beginning to understand how homesteading fostered the character of the West, how people who chose to uproot everything, travel by foot and horse and wagon to work a land for five years with nothing but the promise of ownership would feel about their land and about their right to autonomy.

Added to those who got their land by the book were people who were a bit more, shall we say, circumspect. Instead of filing a claim through the proper channels, Bill Menor moved in and squatted on the land he wanted. It worked out for Bill, however, because after sixteen years he was able to secure legal title. During that time, he built the ferry, a well, and a general store. Bill's brother, Holiday, joined him, but one day the siblings had a particularly divisive argument and Holliday ended up moving across the river. As Holiday used to say about the two of them, he was "mean, but his partner was Menor."

We learned this from a charming married couple who were volunteers for the Grand Teton Association. Iris, from New Jersey, and Ken, from Georgia - originally. Hints of their accents remained as they told us about Jackson Hole weather. The couple liked to sit on the porch at Dornan's and watch the storms barrel in and then roll right by just as fast. Dornan's sat across the Snake River from Menor's Ferry and was a resort with cabins, restaurants, a trading post, a gas station, coffee and ice cream, mountain bike rental, canoe and paddle boat rentals, a wine shop, and a gift shop. The resort is owned by the Dornans, a couple in their 60s, and the family's owned it since before Jackson Hole became part of Grand Teton.

When the Dornans want to retire from the resort, "they could sell to anybody," said Iris. "You, me. Anybody." But, an anonymous donor stepped in, donating enough money to the Grand Teton Association to allow the non-profit to buy Dornan's and make it part of the park.

Now that sounded familiar.

Would it happen? We didn't know. But we did know that there

seemed to be lots of stewards of this land, making sure it would be there, pristine, for future generations.

We walked back to Jeannie the Jeep. Next door to the parking lot, church was in session at The Chapel of the Transfiguration. We'd forgotten it was Sunday (days of the week don't mean as much when you're on the road). As we neared the chapel we met a skinny boy in a blue hoodie, about ten-years-old, I guessed, who was being pulled here and there by his dog. We got closer and the dog checked us out.

"Don't worry. He wouldn't hurt a fly," the boy said. "A dog and a bee, but not a fly."

I could bottle him up.

His parents were in the chapel and the boy was taking care of Buddy, a mix of beagle, pit bull, and about four other breeds he rattled off as his best friend sniffed the scrub brush. Church let out, and after saying goodbye to the loquacious youngster and his Buddy, we entered the ebb and flow of parishioners and tourists exchanging places.

Inside was dark, and at the end of the log structure, a window framed a cross against the bright backdrop of the Tetons. It was about the most majestic setting for a church one could imagine. If you're the church-going type, sitting in one of those rough-hewn pews and seeing the pastor backlit with the mountains behind him in shining detail as he speaks his faith couldn't help but move you, no matter what your denomination.

Driving through Jackson, Wyoming, was like driving through a pinball machine. Bells and whistles everywhere tried to distract us, but we had to keep our eyes on the prize:

Arco, Idaho.

Now what, you may ask, is in Arco, Idaho?

We had no idea.

That's not entirely true. We knew that the EBR-1 Atomic Museum was there. We also knew Arco was just about halfway between Grand Teton and Caldwell, Idaho, or at least it was the closest thing to halfway we could find along that stretch.

My road trip methodology, as you might have guessed by now, is a combination of defined destinations with random routes in between, a healthy dose of good luck fueled by optimism, and the belief in local guidance.

Basically, it's a crapshoot.

We entered our seventh state on our twelfth day. We'd traveled more than 2,400 miles and spent over 60 hours in the car. We'd camped eight of those nights, and with the exception of our two nights in Yellowstone, each time we'd set up our living arrangements, from scratch, only to break them down again the next morning. Every few days we'd find a grocery store to stock up on things that would be easy to cook over a fire or a Coleman stove or to toss in a bowl: pre-seasoned meats, canned beans, bagged salads. Packets of ramen soup contained quick-cooking noodles that could be transformed with my bag o' spices. Breakfast was often eggs and bacon, and while they lasted, I'd rejuvenate one of those pitas we'd picked up in Iowa City by searing it in the grease. Lunch was trail mix or wraps lined with nut butter. Afternoons were spent on the road, and we inhaled the whizzing world like a couple of cats given tuna for the first time (or any time, really).

We were exhausted. We were exhilarated.

It didn't matter if it was a crapshoot or a perfectly executed itinerary. This was America. This was what we came to see.

We came out of the mountains and through Idaho Falls on US-20, a road we could have driven all the way from Elgin. That morning, we'd awakened under cottonwoods. By afternoon, we were driving through lava fields. We pulled into EBR-1 Atomic Museum. Its parking lot sported freshly-painted lines and was ringed with massive Mad Max-like equipment.

There's something about the light in Idaho. It feels like the sky is touching you. The red rocks and green scrub brush sit faded like a vintage Christmas card. A sixty-year-old lead-shielded locomotive with its washed-out paint seems alive, and the yellow lines in the parking lot leap out like a 3-D movie.

We walked past a guard shack and entered the world's first nuclear power plant.

It's deactivated, of course, and has been since 1964. Even so, I grew up in the 70s and 80s, and the idea of a civilian entering a nuclear facility was just wrong. My Cold War-era sensibilities kept thinking "should they be showing us this?" even though there was a sign that said "Cameras are allowed." The guard shack, the nondescript building, the interior all reminded me of a James Bond movie, down to the gauges with their frozen needles and the slate gray panels hiding all the stuff that could make us go boom.

I might have an overactive imagination.

Especially since the facility itself did not build weapons. It was a power plant built to prove Enrico Fermi's theory that atomic power could produce more fuel than it used: EBR stands for Experimental *Breeder* Reactor.

He was right. The museum tells the history of the facility and the science behind it. We took the self-guided tour and learned that atomic energy was harvested on December 20, 1951 when the reactor powered four lightbulbs. The next day, it powered the whole building. Fermi's theory was officially proven in 1953 when the reactor generated more energy than it consumed.

Before leaving we checked out the gargantuan rusting remnants

Lead-shielded locomotive designed to transport nuclear engine

around the parking lot and discovered they were leftovers from an aborted nuclear jet program. After ten years and a billion dollars - yes, billion - JFK scrapped the idea.

Arco, Idaho, with a total area of 1.07 square miles and a population of under a thousand people has five motels. We pulled up in front of the DK Motel, a U-shaped cluster of dusty-blue cabins with a building in the center. As we entered the parking lot, we noticed a hill covered with huge numbers across the street. After ringing the bell to the center building, a young woman with a red nose and a puffed face opened the door. She let us in to the lobby and we could tell it was connected to her apartment. She was as sweet as could be, and we felt terrible for the young woman because she was obviously suffering from an exponentially worse version of the cold I was experiencing. We could hear her toddler next door. As the young mother got us set up I asked her about the numbers on the hill, and she told us that graduating classes from the local high school have been painting them since 1920, including her own.

"Only a couple years haven't done it because they couldn't raise the money," she said.

We asked her where to eat and she suggested The Mello Dee Bar & Steakhouse. The brick building was painted cream with a door on the left under a blue sign with musical notes and "Mello-dee" in cursive over the triangular awning. There were a couple of cars out front, but the place still looked deserted. We parked in front of the door to the right and entered under a big sign that proclaimed "STEAKS" in yellow lettering. Inside, a white board listed burgers and other sandwiches. A bearded gentleman came from the back, greeted us, and gently let us know we had twelve minutes before closing time.

Despite the name and the sign, there weren't any steaks at The Mello Dee Bar & Steakhouse. Our dinner prospects didn't look promising, but we were hungry and tired and hadn't seen an option for fast food. We put our faith in the recommendation from the young woman at the motel and ordered a couple of burgers with tater tots. The man with the beard told us we could sit in the bar next door and he'd bring them to us.

We walked through the adjoining doorway into a room lined with dark paneling, found a seat at one of the tall tables, and each ordered whiskey and seven, $3 per. Six locals lined the bar. There was camouflage, profanity, and chain-smoking. One guy bought a round for the rest. They talked about work, about life, and when the man with a gray ponytail down his back got up to leave, the guy next to him squeezed him in a bear hug and said "I love you, man." A black and white hunting dog named Gracie made sure we were OK, and the bartender told us sometimes there were more dogs than people. "Had four huge black labs and a black standard poodle one time," she said, "and they all got along - probably better than people."

The gent from the place next door, which we'd now learned was a different business named Burgers by the Number, entered The Mello Dee with a woman carrying two baskets of food. He sat at another table and she brought our burgers to us, and they were some of the best burgers we've ever had. I am *still* craving them. They were hand-formed and had to be at least half a pound, probably bigger. I asked the woman how big they were, and she held up her small hand and turned it back and forth. "I don't know. I've never weighed 'em," she said. "The size of my hands, I guess."

We finished our drinks and our burgers and got up to leave, and the men at the bar turned as one and protested. "You can't leave! What've you had, one drink! C'mon!" We thanked them and said we had to go, but have a nice evening.

Outside, we got into Jeannie the Jeep and looked at the sign that said STEAKS. Not promising? I should have known.

DAY 13

Jim hates me.

When Jim gets a cold, it's a beast. It's a nearly apocalyptic event that never ends. It goes on, and on, for days. If he's only ill for a week, it's a short one.

When I get a cold, it sticks around for one day, three at the most.

This cold was a two-and-a-halfer. We'd picked up some cold medicine the day before, and with that and my whiskey, I woke up feeling almost fit-as-a-fiddle. What a relief. It wasn't like I could take a sick day or stay in bed for hours. Plus, we had two stops to make before I would meet some of my in-laws for the first time.

One of the reasons we stayed in Arco, besides EBR-1, was that Craters of the Moon National Monument was a mere twenty minutes past the tiny town. The landscape is 618 square miles of molten vomit. There are 25+ volcanic cones and 60 lava flows, and some are only 2,000 years old. Christianity is older.

I think by this point we've established that Mother Nature is capricious and there's no rhyme or reason to her vagaries. Yes, yes, we know there are scientifically documented explanations for her often seemingly inexplicable creations, but let's just say that when you're driving through central Idaho and come across a sea of black basalt you might be forgiven for thinking, "dayum - that lady was trippin'."

The name "Craters of the Moon" was coined in 1923 by Geologist Harold T. Stearns in an effort to garner protection for an area that contained nearly every type of basaltic lava known to science. NASA took Stearns' sobriquet literally, and in 1969 sent the Apollo 14 mission astronauts to the lava fields because the volcanic activity was supposedly similar to the moon's. As of 2018, NASA was still researching and conducting experiments in this unearthly landscape.

We hiked the short - very short - North Crater Flow trail before driving the Loop Road. Lone pine trees grew in the middle of black fields, and flowers poked their petals through black cracks. Hikers climbed a giant

black dune called Inferno Cone. Tufts of green brush and purple blossoms dotted the black terrain, fed by the rain that had seeped into the lava below.

Originally I'd thought of camping in this harsh and unforgiving world, but as I looked around us, I was glad we'd stayed in Arco. The motel had a tiny shower in a tiny room, but it had a shower, and after the three previous nights of primitive campgrounds, I was sure Jim's family would appreciate our choice.

During our southwestern exploration of the U.S. in 2017, we'd encountered Great Sand Dunes National Park. It was a stumble that made me feel like I knew nothing of my country. Sand dunes, in the middle of Colorado? How did I not know about this? It wasn't like they were hidden. They were preserved as a National Park, for Pete's sake.

When I was planning our drive across the northwestern states, I knew our route would take us from Grand Teton in Wyoming to Caldwell, Idaho, and I discovered we'd drive past such interesting waypoints as the first nuclear power plant, a molten landscape, and Bruneau Dunes State Park.

I felt a similar disconnect. Dunes? Dunes, in Idaho?

We left the black basalt of Craters of the Moon and headed west to the barren Idaho high desert. Three hours later we saw the dunes to our left. We turned and drove towards the piles of sand left behind after the Bonneville Flood some 14,500 years ago. It was a displaced Sahara. Two dunes rose from the center of the basin, a unique formation in the United States since most accumulate at the edge. The biggest peak towered 470 feet high, the tallest freestanding sand dune in North America. A couple of cattail-rimmed lakes at the base of the dunes invited fishing, and we saw a grandfather and his grandson readying their poles. We followed the path to a sundial placed by the local Girl Scout troop near the only public observatory in the state. Jim stood in the center of the sundial and we confirmed that it was, in fact, accurate, and it was time to go.

I felt a bit dissatisfied when we left. There was more to see. There were paths to follow. There was so much sand.

They would all have to wait for another time.

We drove northwest, skirting Boise until we got to a small town. It doesn't matter what town; just that it was small, and family was there. We pulled up to an assisted living facility, met Jim's cousin, Cheryl, now my cousin also, and she took us to see her mom. Jim's aunt didn't recognize him. We didn't stay for long, and I don't know if she ever really remembered him, but she understood he was her nephew. She asked Jim if he'd sing with her, and they sang her favorite hymn, together. The look on her face, and the emotion in that room, was pure joy. When the song finished, they smiled together. Cheryl and I smiled. And when we left, his aunt hugged me with a strength I recognized from the family I'd come to call my own. Cheryl called it the Goodrich hug. Jim called it the Aeschliman hug, after his mom's side. Didn't matter who called it what, that hug was family.

On the way to Cheryl's house I was consumed by conflicting emotions. There was grief, realizing that Jim hadn't seen his aunt for twenty years and that I'd never get to know the person he remembered, compounded by the loss of his other aunt shortly after we'd started our journey. There was gratitude, that they'd been able to sing together and experience real joy.

And then there were horsies.

I'm a happy person. My grandma loved to tell people how, even as a baby, I'd wake up happy. It can be quite annoying for anyone around me, especially first thing in the morning. (Jim will verify this.) I'm frequently giddy and entirely lack subtlety. I "squeee." A lot.

This is my default state. But then I get near horses and it's magnified. Suddenly I am twelve-year-old me screeching HORSIES!!!! and I start to tear up because I'm so overcome with happiness and glee and oh-my-word-they're-so-beautiful. I'm grinning right now at the mere thought of these gorgeous, graceful, imperial beings.

Jim warned Cheryl ahead of time. Cheryl and her husband, Tosch, breed and board thoroughbred horses. Cheryl, being the smart cookie that she is, immediately saw this as an opportunity for help with her evening chores. I, being a twelve-year-old girl in love with horsies, bounced ever higher as we neared their farm in anticipation that I would be invited to actually feed these glorious equines.

Win-win.

At the ranch, Cheryl and I loaded up the wheelbarrow and scooped the feed into the troughs. Mares and foals followed and surrounded us. Yes, there were foals! Or as Cheryl called them, BABY HORSIES! (She totally gets me.) I couldn't stop grinning. I *can't* stop grinning.

Dinner was burgers, watermelon, and chips and salsa outside, followed by ice cream inside. Tosch regaled us with stories of his youth, including the tale of his time in a home for boys. He was fostered by a man who bred horses. To hear Tosch tell it, that man didn't become *like* a father to the teenager; he *was* his father. I reminded them that I was writing a book and asked what I could and couldn't share, and Tosch said, "If I'm telling you, you can share it."

This was a man who made mistakes and grew from them. He owned them. That's a man to respect.

Plus, he had horsies.

Jim took this photo. He's only slightly jealous of the horsies.

DAY 14

e pitched our tent in their yard, so of course I was up before dawn. My cold was now officially gone. I said good morning to the horsies and watched as a couple of the foals romped. Cheryl joined me and I helped her feed them breakfast.

She left early for work and we shared one of those epic Goodrich/Aeschliman/Carter (my family does it, too) hugs. Jim and I had a long day of driving ahead of us, so we broke down the tent and had a quick bite with Tosch before leaving. I didn't want to go. I would have loved to hear more of his stories and to spend a few hours with the horses. Like the cattle ranchers we'd stayed with in South Dakota, this was a different lifestyle from my own, and both families had a distinct feeling of purpose and place. Glimpsing their worlds was a gift.

We crossed into Oregon - our eighth state! - and soon entered Vale. If we'd headed north at that point, we would have been on the Oregon Trail. Instead, we drove through the town on US-20 and noticed mural after mural, even passing a group of artists who were bringing one of the scenes back to life. Some entrepreneurial-minded residents started the "Outdoor

Art Gallery" in 1992 in an effort to bring attention to Vale and highlight its history as the first Oregon stop on the frontier thoroughfare. Twenty-six years later, the gallery was still going strong.

After another hour or so on the road we pulled over in the middle of nowhere. Technically, nowhere is the middle of nowhere, since everywhere is somewhere, but we hadn't seen anyone or any services in miles. We turned a bend and found a pullout in a valley next to a river. We got out to stretch our legs and felt completely isolated. Jim could barely keep his eyes open, so I offered to drive. For the next two hours he slept as I followed the two-lane west through wide open spaces and big skies. Not much grows there. In the 1800s that part of Oregon was known as the Great Sandy Desert, even though there's no sand. It's what the Craters of the Moon area might look like when it grows up.

We arrived in Bend and checked into Motel West. I'd booked it that morning using a site that decides where you stay based on your choices of price, general location, and amenities. On the outside, it was your typical motel: outdoor entrances, second floor rooms reached by a switchback stairwell, buzzing ice and vending machines in the alcove that housed the stairs. Inside, however, we found a recently renovated room with contemporary furnishings, a remodeled bathroom, and new (and working) appliances. It was a real treat, and we would have liked to order delivery and lounge for the day, but I wanted beer.

Bend's inclusion on our itinerary was mostly because of its proximity to Crater Lake National Park. That landmark was our destination for the next day, and Bend was less than two and half hours away. I say "mostly," since we also chose Bend because it's the home of Deschutes Brewery, one of my favorites. However, because we could get their beer in Illinois and we wanted to put our fates into the hands of the locals, we decided to leave the known quantity for last.

We found a place called Cabin 22, bellied up to the bar, ordered some pork rinds and nachos, and asked the bartender where to go. He gave us a few suggestions, and after buying a bottle of Cabin 22's rich and smoky hot sauce to go, we crossed the street to Goodlife Brewing. Despite being Tuesday afternoon, the place was packed and we were lucky to find a couple of seats with a view of the tanks in the next room. We tried a flight and struck up a conversation with another local, Ray, who sold insurance. Ray loved Bend, and with his suggestions and the bartender's from Cabin 22 we had enough places to keep us busy for a week. We only had an afternoon, so we went to Spoken Moto, the place Ray seemed to like the most. It wasn't a brewery, but they had a selection of great beer and a cool vibe. (This was

Bend, so I expected the latter.) As we sat at the bar I looked up camping at Crater Lake and discovered the campgrounds wouldn't open until that weekend.

So, I did what anybody who travels by the seat of their pants would do: I asked another local.

The bartender at Spoken Moto was a 20-something fit blonde who I pictured scaling rocks when she wasn't pouring pints. She told us, without hesitation, that we should go to Diamond Lake State Park. "OK!" we agreed, and left her a hefty tip.

Our final stop was Deschutes, and I have to confess that it was my least favorite. There was nothing wrong with it; it just seemed like a tourist destination (duh) and we were searching for purely local hangouts. I recognize the irony: Deschutes had been our tourist destination. It brought us to Bend, and because of that we explored three other businesses that, combined, gave us insights into the character of the place and the kindness of its characters.

We ended our exploration with a Bend-only Deschutes and headed back to our local motel for an evening of pizza and sleep.

DAY 15

I have come to the conclusion that I am a living example of B. F. Skinner's operant conditioning theory, especially of positive reinforcement. That's the only way to explain my new-found comfort in chaos, lack-of-planning, and ability to throw all caution into the dumpster.

Wait - is that why this trip began in front of a dumpster? Was it just an obvious metaphor? Was Jeannie the Jeep *actually* Skinner's box?

Doesn't matter. What *does* matter is that I let go of my rigid list-making and obsessive researching and trusted that it would all work out. It had on our last big road trip. One example: in Utah we met a loquacious ranger who provided some of our most memorable experiences. Then, on this journey, multiple times we asked locals for advice and by doing so, we learned of places we never would have discovered on our own. Each time we let go and trusted, it worked out all right, and it reinforced the notion that the world is a decent place, people are kind, and it would all be just fine.

Day 15 continued that reinforcement.

We checked out of our lovely motel (not an oxymoron) and explored Bend for a bit. We soon encountered a busker, but he wasn't just any street performer. Haiden had completed a summer program the previous year at Berkeley and was a virtuoso on the violin. "Of course," I thought, "because this is Bend, and Bend is awesome." We strolled a couple of blocks and browsed storefronts and historic plaques. Before leaving, we filled my growler at Goodlife Brewing. We decided we definitely needed to return to this active and vibrant town.

We didn't know what to expect at Diamond Lake. We had the word of the lady who'd poured us a beer the day before, but other than that? Nada. We drove and picked up the Volcanic Legacy Scenic Byway. Along the way, we listened to 80s music and grumbled about gas prices. Even though Jeannie the Jeep was fairly efficient, we still had to feed her once a day. It was like having a third person with us. Not a child, because a child could be placated by smushed peas and pummeled fruit or a foil packet with a tiny straw. No, this third person would be the uncle you never claim whose maw swallows children whole. Every gas station we saw was a *Harry Meets Sally*-like recitation of price-per-gallon callouts. In between, I was singing along to the soundtrack of my teens. The Clash, Phil Collins, Dexys Midnight Runners. I felt for Jim, the professionally trained vocalist, but not enough to stop singing. We were climbing a hill, and "Come on Eileen" came on, and as we neared the apex the tempo increased and I was howling "too ra lu rye aye" and unless you became a teenager in the 80s you have NO IDEA what I'm talking about. But Jim did. He knew right then exactly what my teenage years were all about.

(And we're still married.)

The gas stations disappeared, replaced by pines. We rounded a curve and caught a glimpse of a lake in the middle of evergreens.

"Oh, wow; we're camping there, honey!"

"Uh huh."

Jim, the Montana Man, was all like "I grew up with mountains so this is what I expected" and I, the Midwesterner, was all like "OH MY WORD THIS WORLD IS AMAZING LOOK AT HOW BLUE THE LAKE IS CAN I JUST LIVE HERE FOREVER."

Just kidding - he thought it was pretty amazing, too, especially when we found a campsite on the edge of that lake with a white-capped mountain on the opposite shore.

We set up our tent and stopped at the Diamond Lake State Park information center on our way out. It was supposed to be a quick peek. At first it seemed like it was going to be super quick because we couldn't tell if it was open. Then I saw a figure in the window of the cabin and we tentatively stepped inside, where we met Justin and Jordan - who just happened to be from a town about 40 miles from our former home.

Of course they were.

We started by asking them about hiking and one thing led to another and before we knew it, we'd found out the young couple had sold their home in Highland Park, Illinois, so they could travel. They'd been tooling around for over a year when they ended up as volunteers in Diamond Lake State Park. When we told them we learned about their park because Crater Lake wasn't open yet due to snow, Jordan told us it had snowed two days before we'd arrived. Fortunately, the snow had already melted, or that would have been some mighty cold camping.

The couple then shared a story about a man they'd met recently who'd talked about Glacier. Justin and Jordan told him they wanted to visit that National Park in August. The stranger told them they didn't need to worry because the snow wouldn't come until October 17. "That's very specific," Jordan said to him. "Are you in touch with whoever has their finger on the snow button?"

They didn't really get an answer for that. I hope they made it; the wannabe weatherman was a bit off, since the first snow fell on August 27.

Being fellow Midwesterners, Justin and Jordan didn't know much about life in the wild west. During their ranger training, they asked what they could tell people about coyotes, which are fellow residents of Diamond Lake. The answer was: "If you've walked a trail, you've probably passed a few."

"Well, that doesn't help me! What am I supposed to tell hikers?" Jordan asked.

"Roll stones down the path," the park officials said. "It helps confuse coyotes." Pause. "And bears."

The first time they went hiking, Jordan picked up every stone she could find and loaded her pockets until they nearly burst, throwing them down the path as they hiked. She still stuffs her pockets, and advises fellow hikers to do the same. "It's like weight training," she joked.

Speaking of hiking got us back to the original reason we'd entered the cabin, and we told them about our love of waterfalls. I might have looked at Jim with a bit of adoration as I recounted our engagement story... Jordan excitedly grabbed a brochure featuring a whole lineup of waterfalls we'd pass on our way to the coast the next day. We thanked her and Justin profusely and walked out smiling and shaking our heads. Another day, another round of helpful strangers.

We were back on the Volcanic Legacy Scenic Byway, a 500-mile route with one end at California's Lassen Volcanic National Park and the other at Crater Lake. Nobody was at the entrance to the Oregon park, so we sailed in, passing rows of fire-stripped trees. Like the woods at the base of Devils Tower, fire was a regular and necessary occurence in this forest. Soon piles of snow dotted the hill, and as we drove higher, the piles grew bigger and closer until they merged into one.

I'd seen photos of Crater Lake National Park. The lake was a blue so saturated I doubted it could be real.

It was.

We stepped onto the rim of an ancient volcano and looked at the deepest lake in the United States and the second deepest lake in North America. That depth, and the fact that the water comes solely from rain and snow, is why it's so blue. Crater Lake is considered one of the cleanest lakes in the world, and looking at it makes you feel like you're witnessing purity.

The unreal colors of Crater Lake

It's so blue that its second name was Deep Blue Lake (1853) and its third name was Blue Lake (1862), and it's so majestic its fourth name was Lake Majesty (1865). It wasn't called Crater Lake until 1869 when Jim Sutton, a Jacksonville newspaper editor, decided to explore it by boat and then wrote about it. Why so many names? It seems various explorers encountered the lake, named it, and then forgot about it. I have a feeling it was like Yellowstone's geothermal wonders; nobody believed it was real. It took a journalist to make a name stick.

The first name had a bit more longevity. About 7,700 years ago, Mount Mazama blew its top. It had been a much taller volcano, but then it exploded and the top crumbled, leaving a shell of its former self that filled with water. The Klamath tribe witnessed this event. In their lore, the below-earth Llao fought the above-earth Skell. Skell won, the mountain collapsed, and the lake was born. They called the lake Giiwas and considered it a place of power.

We stood on the rim with a lone man wearing a photographer's vest adorned with pockets covering every available space. Tourists roamed and took their selfies and climbed over gnarled roots. The three of us - Jim, the photographer, and I - made our way towards a neon green tree shooting out over the bluest of blue waters. I carefully picked my way down a gentle slope and framed my photos. I exchanged places with the lone man, and we made some commiserating comments about the intensity of the colors. Jim followed after him. We (Jim and I) took our own selfie. It was a moment to be marked. To say: "We were Here."

It was 6:30 when we returned to our campsite. We still had plenty of light. It was mid-June in the west, and the sun wouldn't set for a couple of hours. I sat in my camp chair by the lake with a roaring fire at my feet. I wrote in my journal, drank some beer from Bend. I was content.

DAY 16

og shrouded the lake. It was quiet. I felt like a thrashing giant as I walked up the hill to the bathrooms. The walk back down wasn't quite as loud, and I began to see details through the dissipating mist. Gradually, I glimpsed Mount Bailey across the water. In the short time it took to make our breakfast of bacon, eggs, and strawberries, all that remained of the fog was a thin strip of white dividing the mountain's peak and base.

Diamond Lake. Contender for best view from a campsite.

Today, more than two weeks after we had begun our journey, we would reach the coast. In sixteen days we'd driven nearly 3,700 miles and spent more than ninety hours in the car. We'd already had an unending string of incredible experiences and we weren't even to the halfway point.

Part of me was ready. But at the same time, I didn't want to be halfway through our trip, because that would mean that every mile was closer to the end than the beginning. When I thought about the end, I also had to consider that we had no home.

That thought was best left for another day.

This day was meant for waterfalls.

We packed up and moved out, waving at the two couples in the neighboring campsite who were loading up their van. We stopped at the information center in the hopes of saying thank you to Justin and Jordan, but it was their day off, so we left and followed OR-138. The "Thundering Waters" brochure that the rangers had given us listed 25 waterfalls in the vicinity, and we would be able to easily visit four of them on our way to the coast.

The Cascade Mountains overflow with waterfalls because the range is a string of volcanoes that belched lava over the course of several thousands of years. Some of the lava formed into resistant, or hard, bedrock, and some of the layers were softer. Lava's porous, so that meant there were also lots of creeks, springs, and rivers. If you've seen a canyon you know that water's a persistent lady. In this neck of the country, she'd flow over a hard layer of bedrock one drop at a time and pick away at the layer underneath until the softie gave up. Then she'd plunge down to the next resistant band, land in a pool, and continue downstream. Eventually the rushing water would eat the top layer of bedrock, too, and the plunge would move further upstream. The whole process takes an awful lot of time, though. To give you an idea, Niagara Falls is one of the fastest moving waterfalls in the world, and it still took 12,500 years to recede seven miles.

We moved a bit faster than that.

We pulled into the lot for Clearwater Falls and, noticing their van, realized we were now following the people we'd passed in the campground. The hike to the falls was short and we quickly met up with the four of them. They asked us to take a photo of them and we asked them to take a photo of us. Their dog trotted back and forth, investigating the four of them and the two of us.

The setting for all of this activity was a fairytale of fallen trees, criss-crossed above water that cascaded over a staircase of velvety, moss-covered rocks. It was the very definition of verdant. I kept looking for elves and gnomes, and I even thought I might find a troll or two. I almost cried.

A soft-spoken woman, one of the four people we were now following, pointed out a mound of sawdust about a foot below a horizontal log. "See what's making it," she prompted, and I immediately felt she might be a

Top - Clearwater Falls; Bottom - Deadline Falls; Right - Whitehorse Falls

teacher. I peered at a small hollow in the wood and saw an ant, and then another and another. One by one, the insects emerged from the depth of the log with tiny pieces of pulp in their pincers, and then teetered at the edge to drop their cargo. Below, fellow ants picked up the pulp, piece by piece, and carted it away. This was an ant's version of "how do you eat an elephant?"

Clearwater Falls was a segmented waterfall. Our next stop, Whitehorse Falls, was a punchbowl. We learned this from the Thundering Waters brochure, which described the various types of waterfalls one could find in Umpqua National Forest. Given some time I might be able to pick the various types out by sight, but that day all I noticed was that Whitehorse was a short fall from a narrow stream that plunged into a wide, circular pool.

We encountered the two couples again. The black dog, whose name we now knew was Jazz, came over to say hello a few times in between her exploration of more moss-covered rocks. It was yet another fairytale setting, a lush, sensuous environment. Jim and I continued our tradition of kissing and saying "yes," but now each sappy moment was accompanied with laughter at how ridiculous we were. Seriously - how many waterfalls had we seen on this trip? When we kissed at Smith Falls in Nebraska our little routine was infused with romance. It wasn't like we ran into waterfalls every week in Illinois, and Smith Falls had been our first on this trip. But now? It was like Oregon was testing us. "Still saying yes? Yeah, well what about now? Are you suuuure? 'Cause here's another one!"

"Yes, yes, a thousand times, yes!" was getting to be quite literal.

We drove further west and found Watson Falls. At 293 feet it's the third tallest waterfall in Oregon. The trail had an elevation gain of 370 feet. I remembered a time that figure would have intimidated me. It's a good thing that fear was in the past, because the trail was one dazzling view after another, and despite that continual uphill climb, it didn't feel strenuous. Part of the ease of the hike was sheer wonder at the beauty that surrounded us, but I attribute a good portion of it to Jazz. We'd climb a few steps and she'd be there waiting for us, her tail wagging her whole body. Then she'd run up ahead until we rounded another turn. We couldn't even see her people. She guided us all the way until we caught up with the two couples, and even then she stuck around until they called her to go.

About halfway up we met a man and a woman resting on a bench and we joined them for a bit. Bill and Jane from Indiana had been to this area twenty years ago and vowed they'd return. They'd recently retired and were pulling an RV with no real plan, just visiting the places they remembered and exploring others they'd always wanted to see. It was a dream they'd had, and they made it real.

Skirting some teenagers who were on their way down, we made it to the top of the trail. It was a bit muddy, probably from the snow that had fallen a few days before and had now melted, so we stayed back far enough from the edge that we wouldn't slip. More of the ubiquitous moss covered every visible surface at the base of the falls. Magical.

Reluctantly, we trekked back down, careful to avoid sliding on the pine needle-strewn path.

Our fourth and final waterfall of the day was an hour west. We followed the North Umpqua River to Deadline Falls, a short and thunderous block waterfall. From the lot, we walked a quarter mile trail through ferns and old-growth forest. Emerging at the shore of this Wild and Scenic River, our third on this trip, we wound our way through lichen-covered stones and wildflowers to watch fish jump. I didn't expect to see any, but we waited,

and every couple of minutes a fish, either steelhead or salmon, would leap out of the water in an attempt to continue upstream. They'd come all the way from the Pacific Ocean and we rooted for them to make it over the hump.

We drove west, through Roseburg, up OR-138 until it became OR-38. Stopped at the Dean Creek Elk Viewing Area. We didn't view any elk, but we didn't stay long. I was impatient. We drove west, and then we were on US-101, PCH, the Pacific Coast Highway. We drove north, crossed the Umpqua River, and Jim pulled into the Oregon Dunes Day Use parking lot. He didn't ask; he didn't have to. I sat on the edge of my seat and as soon as he stopped (I think we were stopped), I jumped out like a steelhead and gazed at the Pacific Ocean.

I felt infinitesimal.

Tears blurred my vision as I looked at a coastline of forest and dunes and the mighty sea beyond. The sheer enormity of everything we'd seen in the past sixteen days overwhelmed me. It had been one majestic and awe-inspiring experience after another, and there was still so much more. How could I write about this? How could I share this grandeur, or even think my telling could be remotely adequate? I'll just write it, I thought. I'll just write what I saw and what I felt and hope that it's enough.

DAY 17

" **I**'m sitting in a crappy motel listening to crappy traffic and drinking crappy coffee that I had to get from the crappy office - and I'm loving it."

So began Day 17.

Geographically we were at the halfway point, but in actuality it was a buffer zone. That day we were driving north. The next was when we'd begin the drive home, wherever that was. The immediate plan was to drive up PCH and find a camping spot somewhere in the northwestern corner of Oregon.

It was Friday morning and we'd awakened in Florence. Our crappy motel was the result of a random search that hadn't worked out as well as our previous dart throws, but it had been a place to sleep and cost less than a dinner-and-a-movie night. After we checked in we passed a scraggly-bearded overall-donned man who was sitting in a woven lawn chair outside his room, nursing a stubby cigar. When we left to pick up some dinner we noticed he'd used an orange cone to guard his parking spot, and the next morning we found our motel neighbor had parked perilously close to Jeannie the Jeep. It would have been easy to make assumptions since we didn't get a chance to talk to the man. If we had, you know what? I bet he would have been as kind as a volunteer ranger. There were no scratches on Jeannie, so we chalked the bearded one up as an "interesting" character and turned out of the crappy parking lot.

Driving the Pacific Coast Highway and not stopping at every single town and overlook just about killed me. I gazed with longing at each shack advertising fresh salmon and two-story hotels with weathered siding and this-and-that historic whatever. Every few miles Jim asked if I wanted to pull over, and I'd sob "no, no, we'll see it another time," in a truly pathetic whine.

If you've read Volume 1, then you already know this, but since I'm not sure I've mentioned it yet in *this* book: Jim is a saint.

Our first designated stop was only about twelve miles from our crappy motel. Heceta Head Lighthouse has been guiding sailors since

Heceta Head Lighthouse

1894. Its first-order Fresnel lens, the largest of its type, beams light 21 miles into the sea. It's the brightest lighthouse on the Oregon coast, and one of the most picturesque in the country. Before visiting the actual lighthouse we stopped at an overlook and watched sea lions sunning on the basalt. Ravens flew around us, their blue-black flapping wings distracting from the rotating beacon across the bay. We drove down to the parking lot, which abutted the beach, and walked uphill. We passed the former lighthouse keeper's home, which was now a Forest Service-run bed and breakfast. I would have loved to have stayed there instead of the crappy motel, but the rate for one night was about half of what we spent on gas for the entire trip.

We climbed towards the lighthouse and came across a lady named Toni reading one of the wayside markers. She told us to keep hiking up the trail and we'd find the absolute best view of the lighthouse. Since she wore a vest blazoned with Volunteer, we followed her advice.

At the top of the trail we came eye to eye with that powerful Fresnel lens and acknowledged that Toni was right (always listen to park service volunteers). Like our spot at the rim of Crater Lake, there was room for only one person at a time. I snuck in while Jim struck up a conversation with the volunteer stationed at that point. He found out that Joseph was from Spokane, and we were going to be in that Washington town in just a few days because we had family there.

Top - Volunteer; Bottom - Best view ever of Fresnel Lens

I switched places with Jim so he could see the view. "What brings you out here?" Joseph asked me.

"I'm a travel writer," I said.

"YOU! You travel writers!" he said. "You've got to stop telling everybody our secret places! There's a reason they're secret!" And then he proceeded to tell us his secret places. Toni had joined us by this time and we learned she and Joseph were married. She told us she was a California girl and the couple volunteered one month at a time, working three days on, three days off. We spent more time talking with them than we did looking at the view or learning about the lighthouse. It was an excellent decision. (And no, I'm not sharing their secret places. I promised.)

As we left we passed under the Cape Creek Bridge, a double-tiered structure reminiscent of a Roman aqueduct. When we drove over Alsea Bay I began to notice a similarity in the bridges along the coast. Turns out they were designed by the same man, Conde McCullough. The designs are distinctive, with arched steel painted green and art deco concrete columns. Built between 1921 and 1936, they bring a sense of unity to the drive, making 101 through Oregon not just a means of getting from one place to another, but also a destination itself.

We drove through the towns along the way, but I couldn't resist the siren call of the ocean, so we pulled over at Cape Perpetua Scenic Area, Seal Rock, the Yaquina Bay Lighthouse, and Cape Foulweather.

Cape Foulweather?

It was a perfect sunny day when we visited, but on March 7, 1778, it wasn't so balmy. That's when Captain James Cook got his first sight of the Oregon coast. The weather was so bad he couldn't get closer than three leagues, or about ten nautical miles. Cook and his crew had left the Hawaiian Islands (which he'd named the Sandwich Islands) more than a month before, and then they finally saw land and couldn't get near it.

Cape Foulweather, indeed.

US-101 turned inland and we drove through a valley, past a flea market in a red barn, past an air museum, and finally arrived at Tillamook County Creamery Association at quarter after five. We browsed their dairy farming museum before joining the line to sample the cheese.

Ah, cheese. If I were a poet, I would write odes to cheese.

Tillamook Creamery is a co-op of local farmers that began in 1909. The cheddar recipe is even older, dating back to 1894. We bought a two-pound block of the extra sharp white, and while I knew I could probably get

Cape Perpetua Scenic Area

it at any major grocery store, when in Tillamook... I figured by buying the cheddar from the source, they'd get all the money instead of having to share it with distributors and retailers.

Jim was more excited about the ice cream. Relatively speaking, that recipe was just a young'un, since it was developed in 1947. My father-in-law grew up in eastern Washington and he darn near insisted that we visit Tillamook for their ice cream. I ordered salted caramel in a cup and Jim ordered huckleberry in a waffle cone. This was to be my introduction to not only Tillamook, but also to the call of frosty treats and the near obsession with huckleberry in the west.

I've had ice cream before. I've even had huckleberries before. Put the two together, at a creamery that controls every step from the cow to the cone, and we were in huckleberry ice cream heaven. I had a slight bit of cone-envy, but that salted caramel was a close runner-up, and it was the saltiest creamiest carameliest I've ever had. I know I can get Tillamook's ice cream at the grocery store, but I don't want to dilute that fantastic culinary memory. We'll just have to go back.

It was nearly six by the time we left Tillamook and we still didn't know where we would be sleeping that night. The original plan had been to camp, but since it was getting late I looked into booking another crappy

Haystack Rock at Cannon Beach; Right - anemones and seaweed

motel. Unfortunately, the cheapest accommodations I could find were in Portland, ninety miles away, at $200 a night. Camping it would be. (Hopefully.)

We drove through a shaded canyon of old-growth forest and I put our sleeping dilemma out of my mind. I knew it would work out. It had to.

We parked in the Cannon Beach public lot. Sunset was near. We didn't see any signs, so we walked towards the ocean and as soon as our feet hit the sand we could see Haystack Rock. The tide was out, and the thin film of water covering the beach mirrored the distinctive basalt outcropping. Here and there we'd skirt a beached jellyfish. Murres, black and white birds with big bodies and tiny wings, cavorted above us like kids at recess. A family rode recumbent bikes with fat tires. A man with shoulder-length curly blonde hair tested pose after pose in front of his tripod. At the base of the monolith, bright green seaweed crowned rocks like discarded Halloween wigs. Starfish and anemones, closed and open, clung to the rocks, and seagulls clomped from one bald spot to the next. Gradually, the tide came in as the sun moved closer to the horizon. We had to get going if we wanted to have any chance of finding a place to sleep, but before we could leave I had to stick my toes in the water. We walked to the incoming

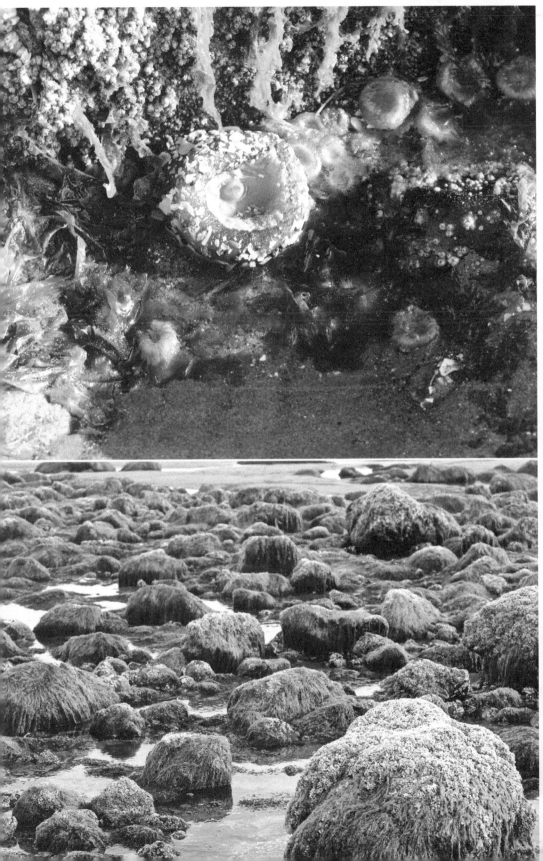

waves and took our shoes off. I screeched as the cold fingers bathed my toes, but I had done it. I'd walked on sand and felt the water of the Pacific Ocean.

We passed a park. Campground Full, the sign said. Then another sign, and another. We reached Fort Stevens State Park, the northernmost park along the coast. Campground Full. It was now past dusk. We saw a sign for an RV park. Full. We circled a park where trailers went to die. The KOA looked promising, and we got in line behind kids buying ice cream and men buying beer. Nope. Full. With what I can only imagine was a look of complete desperation, I asked the young cashier if he had any suggestions. He told us about another RV park that wasn't too far.

Tired, hopeful, we pulled into Kampers West. It was a parking lot of motorhomes. We could tell some of the rigs were transient, but others had sheds and porches. At the end of the rows we found a strip of grass reserved for tents, and there was a single solitary spot. On one side, a family with chairs for him, her, and their toddler finished arranging their campsite. On the other, a couple sat by their fire. We had just enough light to set up our tent.

I knew it would work out.

DAY 18

"Ugh."

"Foot?"

"Growler."

We were now communicating with grunts and one-syllable words.

In case you don't speak Jim and Theresa, my foot had been cramping a little, so Jim thought it was giving me fits. Instead, the growler had fallen over.

The upside of our last-minute campground find was that, like the day before, we were less than fifteen minutes from our first destination of the morning. What we sacrificed in quality we made up for in proximity.

Our current route put us back on the general path of the Corps of Discovery with a visit to Fort Clatsop. It's in the Lewis & Clark National Historic Park, a collection of twelve areas in both Oregon and Washington that highlights the explorers' time in the region. We only had time for one of those areas, so we made it the place where they stayed the longest.

The explorers reached this part of the country, the end of the line, in November, 1805. At first they were on the north side of the Columbia River, but after hearing that the land south of the river was more plentiful, Meriwether and William put it to a vote: should they stay where they were, or should they hope for greener pastures? Remarkably, everyone got a say in this decision, including Sacagawea, their "Indian" scout, and William's slave, York. The entire group decided to go south, and by December 24 the troupe was ensconced in their new fort along the Netul River.

Inside the Visitor Center are displays about the Corps' journey as well as the historical context and information on the Clatsop, the tribe for whom the fort is named. There's a family tree of William Clark's descendants, and I was amazed to see that Clark named his first son, born in 1809, Meriwether Lewis Clark. After two years of forging their way through unknown territory, the fact that Clark still liked Lewis enough to name his kid after him astounded me.

The fort itself is a replica, the second one built on the site. The original had disintegrated in the wet climate and the first replica, built in

1955, burned fifty years after it was constructed. The park service had more information in 2006 than it did when the original replica was built, so the existing one is considered to be more accurate than the first. Stepping inside the rough-hewn cabins, I could picture the explorers hunched over their desks as they meticulously noted everything they'd seen. It even smelled like history.

Fort Clatsop

We took a quick look at the outdoor interpretive center and then walked a short trail to the canoe landing. It seemed like we were barely there long enough to blink, but by the time we returned to Jeannie the Jeep an hour had passed. Fortunately, our next stop was close.

On our drive west two days before, we had popped into the Visit Roseburg Visitor Center to pick up some brochures. While flipping through one of them, I noticed the Scandinavian Midsummer Festival was happening that weekend in the Clatsop County Fairgrounds. What timing! Twenty minutes after leaving Lewis and Clark's fort we were crossing a troll bridge, exploring a Viking Encampment, and listening to an accordion and fiddle duet from Norway.

The festival has been an Astoria tradition since 1968, and in 2017 was designated an official Oregon Heritage Tradition, an honor that's awarded to select annual events that have taken place for fifty years or more. The Scandinavians who attend consider the three-day fest Clatsop County's biggest family reunion. We'd arrived just in time to watch generations of Nordics parade in traditional garb from Denmark, Finland, Iceland, Norway, and Sweden. Each country's folkwear was different, and some of the children were sporting clothes their grandparents and great-grandparents had worn.

In 1870, only 47 Scandinavians lived in Oregon. By 1910, there were nearly 10,000 in Astoria alone, and they comprised 35% of the town's population. Those early immigrants somehow found their way to the mouth of the Columbia River, and they stayed because it reminded them of home.

We'd missed the troll race, but we were able to browse booths of handmade garments and gifts, of swords and axes, of Swedish limpa (bread) and Finnish frikadeller (meatballs). In the Empire of Chivalry and Steel, a man dressed in linen, his cloth made from flax and dyed red with plants and bugs, explained that being a Viking is not your life, it's your job. There were horses from Iceland, a beer garden, and a red-sailed warship. We had to leave as the flag ceremony began, just missing the raising of the five countries' standards.

Troll Bridge at Astoria Scandinavian Midsummer Festival

We crossed the mighty Columbia River into Washington - our ninth state! - and almost immediately, relatively speaking, crossed back again into Oregon. We skirted Portland (and, sadly, Powell's City of Books) on our way to Vista House. The skies turned gray and it began to rain. The timing stunk, since our destination overlooked the Columbia River Gorge. For a mile and a half we followed the steep ten percent grade up to Crown Point. After finding a spot in the nearly full parking area, we walked through a slight drizzle to the hexagonal building. The river, narrow compared to the Mississippi, wide compared to the Rio Grande, curved 733 feet below us.

Inside we browsed a few displays about the history of the Columbia River Highway. There was marble everywhere, and I began to see how the initial funding of $3,812.35 wouldn't quite cut it, even in 1916. When Vista House opened in 1918, the building itself had cost around $70,000, and with its abundance of marble, its green-tiled roof, and its opalescent windows, it looked like it.

An American flag hung from the center of the rotunda. Four terracotta busts of Native Americans stared at it, eye-level. We found a staircase and entered an observation deck filled with smiling, happy people. There were multiple races, multiple languages. A large family took pictures in groups, and everyone jostled to make room for anyone who hadn't been able to take a peek. I hate crowds. It was crowded. But, everyone was nice. Everyone was pleasant. Everyone was respectful. This crowd, I liked.

The rain stopped. As we looked to the east, a hole in the clouds appeared over the Columbia River and the flat gray gave way to hues of green and blue.

Above - Columbia River; Right - Bridal Veil Falls

150

In the early 1900s, scenic drives weren't really a "thing." Of course, that probably had to do with the fact that cars weren't really a thing yet, either. They were fairly new and not the ubiquitous form of transportation they would shortly become. That made the development of the Columbia River Highway farsighted, and it was the first planned scenic roadway in the United States.

Sam Hill was an ambassador of good roads, and Samuel Lancaster was an engineer. Together, the two built a road designed to showcase the scenery. Lancaster found the "beauty spots" first, and then connected them with a 60-foot wide thoroughfare with a grade no steeper than five percent.

We followed the curving pavement, noting the guardrails. Some looked like white picket fences; others were moss-covered stone. Not fifteen minutes after leaving Vista House, we stopped for a hike at Bridal Veil Falls. We followed the short, sometimes steep trail through yet another fairytale forest. If that sounds like I was jaded, I wasn't even close. Because it was overcast, the moss and ferns and leaves fairly glowed. We stopped at a short bridge over a creek that picked its way through black, angular stones. At the viewing platform, a Slavic couple balanced their baby on the railing, and below, a trio of leggings-clad young women posed atop a massive boulder, and everyone was vying for the best shot.

It's understandable. Bridal Veil Falls takes your breath away. There are two tiers, and the water cascades down, down, down, ending at a pool that becomes the creek we'd crossed.

We left Bridal Veil Falls and almost immediately had to exit the Historic Columbia River Highway and get on I-84. After the Eagle Creek Fire of 2017, the old road was closed due to erosion, which caused mudslides and other dangerous conditions. This also impacted Multnomah Falls. It's the tallest waterfall in Oregon, and I'd been looking forward to crossing the picturesque bridge I'd seen in so many photos. Instead, Jim and I joined the throngs at the base and viewed it in its entirety. It made for a short visit, and we were soon on our way again.

The rain had returned when we pulled into our campsite at Viento State Park, but we had a rainfly for our tent and a tall and wide evergreen sheltered the picnic table. Because we'd gotten there early enough, I had time to grill some ribs I'd picked up in Florence along with corn on the cob and black beans and onions. As dinner cooked, a ranger dressed as a beaver stopped by and gave us a sticker. The sky darkened, and then it was dark, and while the fire died we sipped a cup of tea.

Multnomah Falls

DAY 19

Never ever ever ever EVER camp by railroad tracks. EVER.
I know this. Any camper - any *non*-camper - knows this, but when you're driving along the Columbia River and need a campsite, there's no choice BUT to camp by railroad tracks.

When I booked Viento State Park I knew train tracks would border the campground because the Union Pacific Railroad runs nearly the length of Oregon's stretch of the Columbia River. I also knew that I-84 paralleled the other side of the park. I knew it would be loud. But oh, hammer-my-head-in-a-tin-can, it felt like my skull was resting on the tracks. I could *feel* the vibration every few minutes as an engine thundered through pulling 3,489 cars behind it in a snake that rattled for hours (yes, I get the impossibility of that statement and I DON'T CARE), and darn if the engineer didn't have a bullhorn pointed directly at my ear. When it wasn't a train hammering away it was the whine of semis and cars speeding on the highway. It was LOUD.

And yet, despite that torturous night of noise noise noise, the first thing I wrote in my journal was: "It's another beautiful morning on this journey across the northwest. We've been blessed with great, sunny days, with only a couple of exceptions."

What can I say? It was Day 19, and I was at the point where I could either let things get to me, or I could roll with the bad and embrace the good.

The upside to our proximity to the Interstate was that we had a full data connection, so I got a bit of work done from our picnic table. That meant we got a late start, but we didn't have a lot on our agenda besides making sure we got to Walla Walla that night.

We left the campground around 11:30 and continued to follow the Columbia River east. The hills changed colors from the green of the Cascade Mountains to the tans and browns of the semi-arid plains. The Oregon side was still dotted with trees, while the Washington side looked like a watercolor painted with a palette of beige.

We crossed the river. It was another brief hop into Washington. This time, we popped in to see an unusual monument. Maryhill Stonehenge is on a bluff overlooking vineyards, fruit trees, and the Columbia River. It's there because Sam Hill, the same Sam Hill who was responsible for the Columbia River Highway, visited the original Stonehenge in England during World War I and decided to create a memorial on the 7,000 acres he owned in Washington. At the time, people thought the Druids had used Stonehenge for sacrificial offerings, possibly to appease the god of war. Hill was a pacifist, and with the Great War raging he was moved by the symbolism. When he returned home to Maryhill, the name he'd given his land, he built his own version of the stone structure "to remind my fellow men of the great folly of still sacrificing human life to the god of war." He also wanted to honor the men of Klickitat County who lost their lives in battle, and by the time his monument was complete there were fourteen plaques commemorating the local soldiers' deaths. Hill passed away in 1931, two years after the memorial was dedicated, and his ashes are buried in a crypt on the side of the hill.

In 1995, the Klickitat County War Memorial Project Committee refurbished the memorial and built a nearby monument to soldiers who have died in battles subsequent to the War to End All Wars. There's also a small POW/MIA sculpture.

It was a solemn visit. Despite the quirkiness of finding a Stonehenge replica on this quiet hill, what it symbolized deserved respect.

Maryhill Stonehenge

At the top of the bluff we saw a sign for a winery down below, so we followed a barely-paved road, turned a corner at a steepled church, and

Columbia River from Maryhill Stonehenge

drove past orange groves to the Waving Tree Tasting Room. Even though it was Sunday and Father's Day, owners Terrence and Evelyn were pouring wines in the small cabin. This was their retirement plan, they told us. Well, it was his retirement plan. Evelyn had something more leisurely in mind, but for now they were there, producing top-quality estate-grown Italian and Rhone varietals. It's a family affair; Terrence makes the wines and his son Takashi manages the vineyards along with his daughter, Kimiko, who also designs the labels. Evelyn helps out as needed. We took a bottle of Sangiovese to go and wished them luck with their respective plans for their future.

We drove back into Oregon and followed the Columbia River, again, until it turned north, entered Washington, and US-730 became US-12. It was only four in the afternoon when we walked into Seven Hills Winery in Walla Walla, but the lack of sleep from the night before, combined with the previous two and a half weeks, caught up with me. Here we were, in a place with 140 wineries in the region, and I only had energy to try one glass in one tasting room. We walked a few blocks around downtown and gave up. I'd booked a Super 8 for the night, so we picked up a box of mac 'n cheese and figured out how to fix the noodles in the microwave. That and our leftover ribs and we were done. It was just as well. We had a long day ahead of us, but we had no idea how long it would turn out to be.

DAY 20

With a few exceptions, we hadn't been tied to the clock on this trip. But this day, we were seeing someone special who was expecting us at a certain time. Because we had to backtrack a bit for our first stop, we made sure we were up and out early. That's easier when you don't have a campsite to break down, and we pulled into Whitman Mission National Historic Site by nine.

Located a few miles west of Walla Walla, Waiilatpu, as it was known in 1847, was the site of a horrific attack. That year, five Cayuse murdered missionaries Marcus and Narcissa Whitman and nine of their fellow settlers. They also took between 49 and 53 hostages, including many children.

Before the massacre, missionaries and settlers had been following the Oregon Trail, entering the area in rapidly increasing numbers. The migration began in 1836 when Marcus and Narcissa, along with Reverend Henry and Eliza Spalding, made the long journey west from what is now the Midwest. The two couples were missionaries with ABCFM, the American Board of Commissioners for Foreign Missions, and these early pioneers helped establish the Oregon Trail. They were so early that Narcissa and Eliza were the first white women to make the transcontinental journey. Once they arrived in the area, the Spaldings founded a separate settlement and the Whitmans set up their mission in Waiilatpu.

The Whitmans tried to convert their new neighbors, the Cayuse, by teaching them the advantages of an agricultural lifestyle. That didn't work out so well, but the missionaries kept trying. For more than a decade, Marcus and Narcissa ministered to the natives as well as to the increasing number of settlers following the path they helped forge. Then, in 1847, the Whitmans were slaughtered.

Indians killed innocent missionaries who were simply trying to help. At least, that's how the story was told for more than a hundred years. While the massacre was unconscionable, there's a backstory that has only recently become part of the official tale.

The influx of settlers to the area swelled quickly; in 1841 there were

25 pioneers, and by 1847, 5,000 people crossed through Waiilatpu. With these people came disease. It was bad enough that the settlers were taking over the tribes' traditional lands and trying to change their way of life, but then measles struck, and more than 200 Cayuse, half the population, died. Because Marcus was a doctor, the Cayuse blamed him. They thought he was poisoning them.

This thought wasn't entirely unbidden. The ABCFM was Protestant, and its representatives were often competing with Catholics for the souls of the natives. There was a rumor that Joe Lewis, a Catholic missionary, told the Cayuse that Dr. Whitman had been administering poison instead of medicine. Five members of the tribe believed that, and took revenge by killing their alleged poisoners.

The murders temporarily put a stop to the mad dash west on the Oregon Trail. For the next eight years the Cayuse Wars raged, but it was a losing battle for the natives. In 1848, Congress established the Oregon Territory in direct response to the murders, and by 1855 the tribes in the region had ceded most of their lands to the U.S. Government.

It's only been since 2010 that a more balanced telling of this tragedy has played out. The site was originally preserved in 1936 as the Whitman Mission National Monument, a memorial to the slain Americans. It was redesignated a National Historic Site in 1962 and began emphasizing its historical importance as well as its status as a memorial, but it still focused on the Whitmans and pioneer life. Finally, in 2014, the park changed the entrance sign to reflect neutrality. Inside the museum, the exhibits now tell the stories of both the pioneers and the people who were already there.

Covered Wagon on the Oregon Trail at Whitman Mission

History is told by the conquerors, but sometimes the conquerors evolve. We'd learned that at Little Bighorn, and it was reinforced at Whitman Mission.

There's a park in Illinois called Starved Rock. It's a land of canyons, caves, and waterfalls hidden in the prairie. When you're driving on the Interstate you'd never know it's there. You can look out across the plains and have no idea that there are steep drops and bluffs under that flat horizon.

Eastern Washington isn't exactly flat, but coming upon Palouse Falls provides that same feeling of discovery.

This was another place that Jim's dad had (strongly) suggested that we visit. We were nearing my father-in-law's childhood home, and I knew when he said "go there," we should go there. We parked in front of a tiny campground on a hill and approached a chain link fence, careful to stay clear of the edge after seeing signs warning us that four people had fallen to their deaths recently. I could see why. I wanted to get closer to the falls plummeting nearly two hundred feet over basalt cliffs. Near the plunge, a line of eroded rock resembled a row of skyscrapers. The layers of earth in the crater carved by glaciers were stacked like unmortared slabs, as if a mason hadn't quite finished his job, and moss covered the wet stone at the bottom.

Palouse Falls

There are two stories that tell the power of these falls better than I can.

In the first story, in 1984 a utility proposed a dam upstream. The hydroelectricity generated would have provided about a third of the power for the county and would have reduced taxes significantly. But, it would also have destroyed the falls.

The people said no.

The second story involves a bunch of kids. In 2013, students at Washtucna Elementary School thought that Palouse Falls should be the official state waterfall. They proposed this idea to House Representative Joe Schmick when he visited their school. He said, "OK. Write a bill." They did. In December of that year, Representative Schmick presented House Bill 2119 to the Washington State Legislature. It passed unanimously.

The Senate had a couple of fuddy-duddies, but the bill still passed with a 46 to 3 majority. On March 18, 2014, Governor Jay Inslee signed it into law, and Palouse Falls became Washington's official state waterfall.

Eastern Washington is a land of abundance. It's a land known for wheat, and I was about to meet a local wheat farmer known around the world for his innovative farming techniques.

He's also family.

I'd heard stories about Uncle John and his wheat. I'd baked bread with his wheat. I knew that he was a no-till farmer, and I'd been told that he would talk your ear off about farming, if you let him. When we first started planning a visit to see him he offered to take us on a tour, and other family members asked us "are you sure? You'll be out there for hours!"

We were sure, we were out there for hours, and I could have spent more time listening to this passionate, driven man.

When we pulled up to the 1909 barn near Colfax, Washington, we didn't know what to expect. Uncle John's wife was the aunt who had passed away not three weeks before. We let him lead, and he greeted us effusively. We loaded into his truck and he took us through his fields. They'd been his father's fields - Jim's grandfather's - and had been split up among the siblings. Over time some of the fields left the family, but gradually Uncle John got them back, and now he farms 4,000 acres. Knowing that you don't ask farmers how many acres, I was surprised he told us. It wasn't just because we're family; Uncle John is that open.

I sat in front and Uncle John paused now and then to turn in his seat so he could see both of us. He'd point out the soft white wheat, red wheat, Northern Spring wheat. He talked about worms. A lot. "We've got worm castings ten feet deep!" he exclaimed. "Worms are nature's plows!" We drove past the shack where his cousin was born.

He drove the dirt road through fields of canola, pointing at the yellow flowers. "That's fuel," he said. "I burn it in my truck." I got out and the exhaust smelled like french fries. We drove past corn fields. "Corn is like music, man." You can't grow corn in Washington because the soil wasn't up to it, yet there they were, rows of ears in between wheat, canola, and garbanzo beans. "This is like exploring space," he said, "or the bottom of the ocean. We don't know what we don't know. We're just getting started."

Uncle John tours the world to teach no-till farming, and he'll be at it as long as he can. "Retire? You nuts?" he said. "I've been waiting my whole life to see this."

Field of canola in Eastern Washington

We followed the rutted road back to the farmhouse built by Jim's great-grandfather and toured the century-plus old home. After a quick stop to meet Jim's other aunt and her ornery alpacas, Uncle John, Jim's aunt, and the two of us drove into Colfax for Chinese. It was a one-stoplight, two-Chinese-restaurant type of town. We ate at Eddy's, their favorite. The food and the company were so good I forgot to take a single picture.

Alpacas!

Reluctantly, we said goodbye. We had one more place to visit and we were cutting it close. We'd been told that Steptoe Butte offered the best view in this part of the state, and if we missed it, well, we'd regret it. It was nearly nine when we approached the quartzite island and Jim drove as fast as he dared up the rocky one-lane road. We circled around and up the peak, higher and higher as the sun dipped lower and lower. When we got to the top, all that was left was a horizon-length streak of fuschia with a bright ball of yellow in the center.

Sunset from Steptoe Butte

Jim drove in the dark to Loon Lake, about an hour north of Spokane. My brother- and sister-in-law own a home on the side of a mountain and we plugged the address into the GPS. It took us the long way around. Asphalt became black gravel and then it was rough ruts in the steep slope. Street signs were painted boards nailed to poles. Finally, after what seemed like hours, we found it.

We collapsed into a bed in a room in a cabin filled with family. Jim's parents, his sister, her husband - they were all there. His family was mine, and it felt like home.

DAY 21

One of my dreams is to own a cabin on the side of a mountain by a lake. Alternatively, I suppose I could marry a man whose family owns a cabin on the side of a mountain by a lake. Then we can simply show up in the middle of a month-long road trip and not have to worry about silly things like winterizing and stuff.

I slept until somewhere around nine. I took a cup of coffee out on the deck and watched a neighbor kayaking in the still water. Jim got up and we talked with his parents and sister and brother-in-law about Uncle John. We told a few stories from the journey out, and finally, around 11:30 or so, we left for Spokane.

We probably should have left earlier. There were all sorts of museums and things we were supposed to see, but we were tired. Good grief Gertie, as my grandma used to say, we were tired.

Our first stop was a quick visit to Northwest Museum of Arts & Culture to see if we could come back another day. Kate at Visit Spokane had arranged a pair of tickets for us, and the woman at the front desk told us it would be no problem. That left us just enough time to meet Kate at Central Food for lunch. I dug into their PNW Lentil bowl, a healthy infusion of local spinach, lentils, and roasted beets, while Jim ate a smoked ham and cheese sandwich and Kate extolled the virtues of Spokane. Her passion was infectious. When we'd finished eating, we strolled with her along the Centennial Path towards the Spokane Falls. Yes, there's a waterfall in downtown Spokane, because this is the west, and waterfalls are everywhere.

Wishing we had time to ride our bikes, we got back in Jeannie the Jeep and crossed the bridge to Riverfront Park. Jim knew this park. His parents had celebrated their 50th wedding anniversary (pre-me) at Looff Carousel. It was an appropriate location for the celebration: Charles I. D. Looff had created the hand-carved wooden carousel in 1909 as a wedding gift for his daughter and son-in-law, Emma and Louis Vogels. I was happy my dad made Jim and me a gorgeous table when we got married, but a hand-carved carousel? That's an extravagant gift that borders on the obscene. Unless you take into account that the newlyweds owned an amusement

Top - Spokane Falls; Bottom - Tiger from Looff Carrousel

park and that Looff was the guy who built Coney Island's carousel. For almost sixty years, Looff's gift to the Vogels delighted visitors until their Natatorium Park closed. The carousel languished and in 1975 it was moved to its current location.

We weren't sure it would be open. Renovation of the entire Riverfront Park began in 2016 and included a new building for the carousel. Luckily for us, construction on the glass rotunda was completed a month before we arrived.

I expected a slow, stately, leisurely spin. Not on this ride; there's a reason there were straps. I squealed and gripped the pole with both hands and we flew around faster and faster, and every 360 degrees I'd pry one hand free and try to snatch a plastic ring from the dispenser. Jim turned around and grinned. He grabbed more than I did. He was disappointed, though; the rings used to be metal, and if you pulled a brass ring, you won a free ride. Jim always goes for the brass ring.

After a quick stop at Dry Fly Distillery to try whiskey made with Washington wheat, we drove to the Spokane Valley Heritage Museum. It was closed, but we had to be in the area anyway. Jeannie the Jeep needed some attention. We had driven enough miles, around 4,400, that we needed to bring our rental car in for an oil change. Conveniently, we thought, Hertz had an account with Firestone and there was a participating location down the block from the museum.

While we waited, the lobby television broadcast a news story about children being separated from their families at the U.S. border and put into cages. There was an older woman and a younger man in the waiting room, and I heard her say that parents shouldn't put their children in that situation. "It's sad, but it's their fault," she said.

I silently fumed. "Do they think these parents want to be in that situation?" I thought.

It's easy to be judgmental. It's harder to be empathetic. Empathy requires an emotional investment. A willingness to think "what if" and extrapolate beyond your daily experience.

White privilege is real, and so is American privilege.

On our way out I turned to her and said "You don't know their situation. Maybe empathy would be kinder instead of judgment."

I walked outside. I have no idea what her reaction was. I felt sick to my stomach, but I had to say something. Silence meant tacit approval.

We neared the cabin and slowed as a cougar crossed the road.

Before dinner, my brother- and sister-in-law took us out on their boat. A bald eagle snagged a fish and we followed it across the lake as it flew high above the fray, watching it land safely. It was a magical moment that felt like freedom. Oh, the irony.

DAY 22

I napped.

DAY 23

The day before had been a much-needed respite. We didn't sightsee; we didn't hike. We napped. Napping is glorious. Napping on a cushioned swing at the shores of a lake while water softly laps the pebbled beach is glorious with whipped cream on top. It's enough to make you never want to leave. So, we didn't.

At least, not that day.

That day, we relaxed, took another spin in the boat while my sister-in-law water skied, and decided that we really didn't need to leave the next morning. It wasn't like we had a home waiting for us, and we figured we could extend our rental of Jeannie the Jeep for a couple more days. It was important to rest, but it was even more important to spend time with family. While the rest of the year my brother- and sister-in-law live only three hours from our (former) home, Jim's parents are on the other side of the country. So, we stayed. We napped. And on our 23rd day we explored.

Jim's parents joined us for a day in Spokane. We began our tour by returning to the Northwest Museum of Arts and Culture, and when we pulled up we encountered a Virgin Mary statue made out of license plates reclining on a flatbed hitched to a white GMC pickup topped with a gold shell.

We had no idea what to make of that, so we shrugged, parked, and entered the museum. All of the galleries are below-ground and their contents change frequently. When we visited, one gallery detailed items from Spokane's history. Another featured origami. These were no simple swans. These creations were complex sculptures, and it was hard to believe they were made of paper.

In the largest gallery we studied the works of Edward Curtis. The late 19th-, early 20th-century photographer spent thirty years capturing what he considered a vanishing people. During that time, Curtis visited more than eighty Native American tribes and took thousands and thousands of photos. The result was an encyclopedic collection, and he published twenty volumes of "The North American Indian." The compilation is a glimpse of a time and a people that no longer exist - except it's not quite real, and they're still here.

Many critics think Curtis had the right intentions, and to have access to that many tribes indicated that he'd earned some level of trust. The downside was that Curtis painted with a romanticized brush. His subjects became caricatures, like characters in Buffalo Bill's Wild West shows. Native costumes were props, and modern conveniences like alarm clocks were edited out. It was a semi-journalistic, semi-fictional accounting of native peoples who, despite the myth of the "vanishing indian," did not actually disappear.

I could have studied his images for hours. Despite their flaws, the photos were of real people from more than a century before, and they were fascinating. A tour was about to begin next door at a restored Tudor-style home, however, so we walked over to join a small group gathered in the carriage house. We read the displays about life in the early 1900s until the docent led us to the Campbell House mansion.

Campbell House

Amasa Campbell was an Ohio investor who struck silver and lead in Coeur d'Alene, Idaho. He was a wealthy, wealthy man, what today we'd call a one percenter, and his home was a public display of his riches. His wife, Grace, received callers every Tuesday, for only fifteen minutes at a time, in a gilded room near the entrance. Amasa had a Victorian-era man cave in the basement. There were suits of armor in the foyer, servants' quarters, red-flocked walls, and a dining room fireplace framed with blue and white Delft tiles. Poppies positively littered several walls of the house, making one wonder if there was some sort of hidden meaning in the wallpaper, especially when learning the original was enhanced with flecks of glinting, gaudy mica.

Jim's dad remembered visiting the Campbell House when he was a child, but what he saw back then was very different. Amasa died in 1912, and after Grace passed away in 1924, their daughter, Helen, donated the home to the Eastern Washington State Historical Society. As our docent told us, to them it wasn't an historic home; it was just a home, so they used it as a community museum to display items that, at the time, were historical, and that's what my father-in-law would have seen. Restoration to its original glory started in the mid-1980s, long after the Goodriches had left. Now the mansion is a telescope to its beginnings.

We made a brief stop at the Jundt Art Museum to ogle some Chihuly sculptures and paintings before visiting the Bing Crosby House. The crooner's boyhood home was filled with glass cases containing news clippings, posters, awards, gold records, and trophies. The museum prominently displayed Crosby's Oscar, and a child's jukebox sat on top of a table his grandfather had built.

Memorabilia inside the Bing Crosby House

After a quick lunch at Taco Time we tried another visit to the Spokane Valley Heritage Museum, which had been closed on our first attempt a couple days before. The Spanish Colonial brick and stucco building is an anomaly on Sprague Avenue, a busy four-lane street that had once been lined with apple orchards instead of strip malls. Built in 1912 as the Opportunity Township Hall, it had been the center of government for that portion of the valley until Spokane County voted to disorganize the Township in 1974. The hall changed owners a few times, and then the Spokane Valley Legacy Foundation picked up the deed in 2004 for one dollar. The next year the National Register of Historic Places added the building to its rosters, and a few months after that the Spokane Valley Heritage Museum opened.

The museum is a passion project for Jayne Singleton. As she told me, she "let go of a good corporate job so she could do something great." It's small but mighty, and much of its strength is behind the scenes. They've got an extensive database with thousands of records, maps, and primary source documents. When we told her Jim's parents grew up nearby, she took us back to see the archivist. A quick search and she found a record for a J.A. Aeschliman, who must have been one of my mother-in-law's ancestors.

Whoa.

This thrilled Jayne to no end. She said her favorite part of running the museum is connecting visitors with the past, helping them to

Inside the Spokane Valley Heritage Museum

"reminisce, recall, and rejoice in all that came before us." A glass-fronted working telephone exchange tickled Jim's dad. "Have you ever seen one of those before?" he asked me, with wonder in his voice. "I haven't seen one in decades."

None of us expected much when we parked in the tiny lot next to the small building. Boy, were we wrong.

Royal Newton Riblet.

That's not a fancy barbecue dish made with figs, or a nickname for a baby prince or princess. That's the actual name of an inventor who built a house on a hill.

Royal. Newton. Riblet.

Spokane Valley from Arbor Crest Wine Cellars

Our final stop for the day before returning to the cabin was a visit to the house of an eccentric inventor (because, with a name like that, of course he was an eccentric inventor). Riblet invented a square-wheel tractor, a pattern sprinkler system, and a mechanical parking garage, according to the brochure for Arbor Crest Wine Cellars. The winery is located on

Riblet's estate, a 1924 Italianate-style mansion built on a cliff overlooking the Spokane Valley. The inventor designed it himself and included such whimsical touches as a life-size checkerboard game, a croquet court that he'd transform into an ice skating rink in the winter, and a 6,000-gallon swimming pool carved out of the cliff. He married seven times (because, of course he did), and while he built a gate house, he was such a recluse that instead of housing a gatekeeper, he reserved it for the occasional guest.

It's the perfect spot for a winery.

We arrived about half an hour before the grounds closed for an outdoor concert, which gave us just enough time to check out the view. I grabbed a flight of wines and Jim and I sat in one of the outdoor areas while his parents walked around. The wines were worthy, but I expected that, since winemaker Kristina van Löben Sels whet her whistle at Ferrari-Carano Vineyards. It was a remarkable setting, but a cabin by a lake on the side of a mountain was calling.

DAY 24

Our last full day with family was a day of errands. Our trusty air mattress had popped a rib at Viento State Park and I needed to pick up some of Uncle John's flour, so my mother- and sister-in-law and I drove back to Spokane while the guys hung out at the lake. We picked up a new bed and then bought fifty pounds of Shepherd's Grain to share. Lunch was burgers, cheese fries, and shakes in a 50s-style diner. From behind the counter, Brittany from North Carolina, a student at Gonzaga who was in the National Guard, "yes, ma'am-'ed" us through our lunch.

It was relaxing, and fun, and I thought for the gazillionth time how lucky I was to marry into this family. And then, on the way back to the cabin, we saw a doe and a coyote.

In the evening Jim and I packed up and loaded our gear, plus our share of flour, into Jeannie the Jeep so we'd be ready to go in the morning. We didn't want to leave; at the same time, we were anxious to get back on the road. In two days we'd be in Jim's hometown, and in three would be in Glacier. After our extended break it felt like we were near the end of our journey, but we still had another 2,300 miles to go. I was worried about timing. We knew we had to be back by July 3 and there was a lot of ground to cover. Our days of rest and time with family was worth it, though. I don't know how we would have made it without them.

DAY 25

I'm a sucker for a good farmers market. Meeting face to face the people who grow or create the product I'm buying is intimate and feels like a privilege. I especially love finding a market when I'm on the road, and we made it to the Kootenai County Farmers Market in Coeur d'Alene, Idaho, with about an hour to spare before they closed.

We browsed the rust-painted stalls set up in a grove of ponderosa pines. Mulch softened the ground and a musician played bluegrass from a stage. There were baby goats hiding under a table. Jim bought huckleberry tea and I bought herb-marinated goat's milk feta.

Despite the many charms enticing us to stay (baby goats!), we couldn't linger. We were back to our carefree routine and had no clue where we were sleeping that night, so we got a move on. We had a couple of stops to make before searching for camping on the other side of the state and didn't want a repeat of our after-dusk set up in Oregon.

Kootenai County Farmers Market

The oldest building in Idaho was on the way and we stopped to take a peek. In 1850 - 53, Catholic Missionaries and Coeur d'Alene Indians built the Mission of the Sacred Heart. Well, to be fair, from the way the brochure tells it, the Coeur d'Alene did most of the building:

"The Indians dragged in timbers and rafters, then dressed and put them into place all by hand," it says.

Old Mission State Park preserves the church, the parish house, and the cemetery. Our visit was brief, not just because of time, but because there was some sort of retreat happening. Teenagers dotted the park, each sitting alone and either kneeling in prayer or reading from an orange-covered booklet. All the girls wore skirts. A priest sat facing away from the grounds, and one-by-one a youth would kneel and speak to his back.

It felt uncomfortable, like we were intruding, and we took our leave.

Heading east, we pulled off at the Sunshine Mine Memorial honoring the 91 men who died in 1972 when a fire developed in the shafts. It was one of the worst mining disasters in the country, and *was* the worst in Idaho. Jim's parents were co-owners of a Missoula radio station and his dad was news director at the time. Jim's dad co-opted a colleague to take a photo while he flew over the site. He beat the other news outlets by seven hours, and that image was used in all of the AP stories.

Remarkably, the mine reopened just a few months after the disaster. This was the Silver Valley, a stretch from Coeur d'Alene to the Montana border. It's one of the largest silver districts in the world, producing over 1.2 billion ounces since the first claim in 1884. It's where Amasa Campbell and others made their riches. The company Campbell founded, Hecla Mining, is still digging for silver, and finding it.

We left the memorial and soon entered one of the original mining towns. Wallace occupies less than a square mile and every building is on the National Register of Historic Places. Getting that designation for the entire town was an act of self-preservation.

You don't mess with Wallace.

When he was growing up in Missoula, Jim, his parents, and his sisters drove through Wallace quite a few times to see their family in eastern Washington. The last time Jim made the trek was in the 1970s, and he remembered taking the surface streets through the town even though they were on I-90. That's because, at the time, that stretch had the last traffic light on any coast-to-coast Interstate highway. To speed things up through the valley, the Federal Highway Administration wanted to convert I-90 through Wallace into a freeway. Doing so would have demolished most of

the town.

That didn't sit well with its residents, so in 1979 the city leaders got every building listed on the National Register and downtown became an official historic district. I can picture the "take that!" expressions of Wallace residents as the FHWA realized they'd have to build an elevated viaduct freeway instead.

Our first stop in the still-standing town was the Wallace Chamber of Commerce and its open-air mining museum. We explored, talked to the man inside the visitor center, and then entered the time capsule of downtown. We wanted to see the Center of the Universe. I mean, we'd already been to the Center of the World the year before, and on this trip had visited the (almost) Center of the Nation. We certainly couldn't miss the Center of the Universe.

The Center of the Universe is a sewer access cover?

How did Wallace receive this honor? Well, it began with lead in the water. In the early 2000s, the Environmental Protection Agency discovered that the silver mines had caused an environmental disaster. It was so bad the EPA declared a 21-square mile area around Kellogg, Idaho, a Superfund Site. Upon further inspection, the government agency exponentially increased the area of the site to 1,500-square miles, which included Wallace. This would be disastrous for the economy, especially since some people in Wallace thought the lead was naturally occurring and not the fault of the mines. It was 2004, and Mayor Ron Garitone was having none of it. With an idea hatched in a bar (where else) by four residents, it was decided that since the EPA made decisions based on the concept of "if it can't be proven, it must be true," then so could Wallace. In a fit of cheeky pique, Mayor Garitone declared that a sewer access cover was the Center of the Universe, because thanks to the "newly discovered science of Probalism" nobody could "unearth one scintilla of proof" that it wasn't.

Did the EPA learn nothing from the FHWA? Don't. Mess. With. Wallace.

Joking aside, the pollution in the Silver Valley was and is no laughing matter. Many of the valley's residents have serious health problems, with lead levels that still far exceed recommendations.

Jim made sure I didn't get hit by a car while I straddled the sewer access cover. I took my photo of the Center of the Universe and we followed up that excitement with a visit to the Wallace District Mining Museum. They were going to close before we could tour, but we asked the nice lady behind the counter about camping and she told us her favorite spot. We tucked that away and crossed the street to Wallace Brewing, located 80 steps from the legendary sewer cover.

Beer's big in Wallace. In fact, in 1902 the water wasn't fit to drink due to Typhoid contamination, so the town drank beer. (That's their story, anyway.) We tried a couple of different brews and landed on the Red Light Irish Red Ale as our growler fill. While we sipped, a motorcyclist at the bar struck up a conversation and told us how he had ridden from Spokane, Washington, to Whitefish, Montana, to see a local Missoula band - a four hour ride. I'd figured out by now that in this part of the country, where wide open spaces are the norm rather than the exception, driving long distances is just what people do. When you're in a place like Arco, Idaho, and the only grocery store is a Family Dollar, you'll drive an hour to Idaho Falls to run your errands. Then again, they probably think Chicagoans are crazy for sitting in traffic for two hours every morning and evening. (Can't really argue with that.)

With a full growler and a suggested campground, we got back on the Interstate and soon crossed the border into Montana. After seeing multiple hand-painted signs advertising fresh cherries, we succumbed and found a long building with horizontal brown wood siding on the bottom half, vertical mint-green wooden siding on the top half, and tin signs promoting beer, cigarettes, and credit cards all over. As we paid for our bag of sweet cherries, a weathered, lanky man rang us up and told us he packs up about 600 pounds every three days.

"Or maybe half that. I don't know," he said. "It's a lot."

We thanked him for his efforts and ten minutes later were picking out our campsite in Lolo National Forest. Jim set up the tent and I began making dinner. I hadn't cooked in a few days and I felt ambitious, so I made salsa, refried some canned pinto beans with onions and garlic, and pan-fried some seasoned chicken for tacos. Every few minutes, two hunting dogs named Walter and Cleveland would run through the woods from our neighbor's site and check us out. We knew their names because our neighbor would yell "Walter! Cleveland! Get back over here!" in a huge, booming voice.

Funny, the first five times.

After he boasted to his much quieter friend about getting wasted and kicking a different friend's butt at chess, he finally calmed down and we enjoyed a quiet and peaceful night in the woods.

DAY 26

amping is a pain. Set up. Break down. Walk a quarter mile just to use the bathroom. Bring your own roof. Bring your own bed. Bring your own food. Bring your own everything.

But then, you wake up under a canopy of evergreens, hear the world stir, and inhale life.

There's no substitute, and while room service and showers and pillow-top beds have their appeal, sometimes waking up in the woods supersedes any physical discomfort because you are the most physically aware you've ever been.

That was my world, on the 26th day. Emerging from our tent was a rebirth. I had been tired and anxious, but after a few days with family and a night in the forest, I was ready to jump back into this journey.

Tent camping in Cabin City

So was Jim. We were about an hour and a half from where he'd spent the first eighteen years of his life and he hadn't been back since. He didn't say much, because that's not his way, but I could tell he was antsy.

It was nearly eleven when we reached St. Regis. When the Goodriches traveled back and forth between Missoula and Colfax, this had been their pitstop. It was also everybody else's pitstop, and we navigated with the other tourists around huckleberry-flavored treats, huckleberry-scented candles, hats, t-shirts, and an aquarium of trout. It was a riotous and joyful celebration of the American tourist-trap, and if I'd had an extra hundred or so I probably would have dropped it on a plaid robe and moose slippers. I didn't, which is just as well since Jeannie the Jeep still had no room (even less, now, since we were carting twenty pounds of Uncle John's flour). We left without so much as a frosty treat and continued towards the place of Jim's birth.

There was a vibration and an energy radiating off of Jim and he fairly hummed as we neared the outskirts of Missoula. We approached the Smokejumper Visitor Center and he told me how, as a child, he'd been invited to jump off one of the platforms and his parents said NO, in no uncertain terms was he allowed to do that. He didn't remember how or why he received that invitation, but it didn't matter.

We browsed the museum, quickly, amazed by the extraordinary people who jump into fire to save forests, farms, towns, and people. There were many more places Jim wanted to show me, so we left the smokejumpers and landed at Fort Missoula.

Fort Missoula has a colorful past. The U.S. Government built the fort in 1877. Its purpose, like other frontier outposts, was to protect settlers from the tribes whose lands they usurped. In 1888, the 25th Infantry arrived, the same regiment of black soldiers that would later be assigned to Fort Meade in South Dakota. Those Buffalo Soldiers were one of the first regiments deployed to the Spanish-American War in 1898, and they were also sent to Cuba and the Philippines before their assignment in the Midwest.

Soldiers trained at the fort during World War I, but once that conflict was over the place was nearly abandoned. Then, in 1933, the Civilian Conservation Corps made Fort Missoula its Northwest Regional Headquarters. Volunteers trained each summer and then spread out to places like Glacier and Yellowstone. That lasted until World War II, when the Department of Immigration and Naturalization took over.

The first thing Jim and I saw when we began to explore the grounds

The grounds of Fort Missoula from the lookout tower

of the fort was a small gray guard shack and a sign explaining that Fort Missoula had been an internment camp housing Italian and Japanese detainees. The 1,200 Italians were civilians who'd been on boats heading to the U.S., or were hotel employees or marooned workers from the New York World's Fair of 1939. There were about a thousand Japanese Americans who were held, subject to "loyalty hearings," although none were ever charged. For three years, the internees lived surrounded by chain link fences and forty foot tall guard towers. When Italy surrendered to the Allies in 1944, the Italians held at Fort Missoula could either enlist with the U.S. or be sent back home. The Japanese got shuttled to other internment camps until the war officially ended a year later. We'd seen two of those internment camps the previous year, and it was devasting.

Jim had grown up less than a mile away and was never taught about Fort Missoula's history as an internment camp. That could be because the fort was decommissioned in 1947 and was taken over by the U.S. Forest Service, the Bureau of Land Management, and Missoula County. Most likely it was because the fort technically wasn't an internment camp; instead, it was a detention center that imprisoned non-citizens during the war.

We walked the grounds of what was now the Historical Museum at Fort Missoula. Dispersed throughout the grounds was a schoolhouse, a church, a 1900-era cabin, mill stones from a mid-1800s flouring mill, and a root cellar, among other buildings that illustrated what life was like in this frontier town. There was a lookout tower, moved in 1983 from Sliderock Mountain, and Engine #7, a rare locomotive. As we walked, we met a man walking his dog. I don't know if it was our cameras or our friendly hellos, but he invited us into the Trolley Barn.

Engine #7

The building had been locked, but Steve, who we learned was a volunteer with the museum, opened the doors so we could get a look at the restored interurban streetcar that ran from Fort Missoula to Bonner in the early 20th century. Inside, he and Jim lamented the loss of Tower Pizza. The restaurant had been a favorite of Jim's and his sisters', and as soon as he brought it up Steve said "Oh, wasn't that the BEST?!" Sadly, it had closed just a couple of months before we'd arrived. Sounds like I really missed out, because Steve rescued a menu and put it in the museum.

After bonding with Jim over lost pizza, Steve and his dog, Toby, brought us inside the Tipi burner. Jim thinks the structure looks like a shuttlecock. I think it looks like a Dalek. (And that tells you pretty much all you need to know about us.) Either way, it and others like it were the reason Jim remembers layers of pollution. Tipi burners were used by sawmills to burn waste, and they expelling wood smoke into the valley. Now, the burner at Fort Missoula is a harmless display in a museum and it also acts as storage. Steve opened the door and inside was, appropriately for my caroling husband, a red one-horse sleigh.

Is it a shuttlecock or a Dr. Who villian?

It was time for lunch, but first, Jim wanted to see his childhood homes. There were two, and they were much closer to each other than he remembered. He pointed out the hill where kids would slalom down on their bikes and crash in front of his house. He showed me the field where Farmer Perry would pull out his shotgun if they crossed the wrong line - the epitome of "get off my lawn."

We left his old neighborhood and went straight to Hoagieville. Jim had been talking about this place ever since he knew we'd be visiting Missoula, and he was like a kid when he found out it was still there, that they still used carhops, that they still served the original, and that it tasted exactly the way he remembered. There wasn't much to it: a French bun, salami and swiss cheese, lettuce, and their "special Hoagie dressing." I don't know if it was Jim's excitement or it really was that good, but I looked over my bun at him in shock. We paired the sandwich with seasoned fries topped with neon cheese and a huckleberry shake.

I told you - huckleberries are everything.

Our next trip down memory lane was a visit to downtown Missoula. But first, we had to take a spin around their carousel. This didn't exist when Jim was a resident. A Carousel for Missoula opened in 1995 and it was truly a community project. Missoula cabinet-maker Chuck Kaparich started the project in 1991 with four ponies and a frame. Four years and 100,000 hours of volunteer work later, the hand-carved attraction opened along the Grant Fork River.

It's so popular we had to wait about half an hour before we could ride. Remember I thought the Looff Carrousel in Spokane was fast? I had NO IDEA. I swear, if I hadn't been strapped in and holding on for my dear life I would have been catapulted straight out of that jewel box building and across the river. This was no Sunday in the park with grandpa kind of ride; it was a heart-pumping WHEEEEE! kind of ride. Not only was it fast, we reached for our rings from the mouth of a dragon. And, to put the cherry on top, they had a real brass ring.

A Carousel for Missoula

We cooled off from that thrill with a walk around downtown. Jim showed me where his parents' radio station had been. There were two locations, one of which was in the Florence Hotel. Inside a building that's on the National Register of Historic Places was the old On Air sign he remembered.

I don't think I've ever seen that man so happy. (Except for our wedding, of course. But this was close. Very, very close.)

Our visit finished with a bike ride along the Riverfront Trail, stopping to watch kayakers and surfers - in Missoula, Montana. Brennan's Wave is a man-made surf that was built in 2006 as an homage to Brennan Guth, a world-class kayaker from Missoula who died paddling in Chile five years earlier. As we watched, kayakers would spin, flip, and then float back to calmer waters. Wet-suited surfers jumped up on their boards and balanced as the river churned and held them in one spot.

Brennan's Wave - surfing & kayaking in Montana

Worn out just watching them, we ended our day at the motel curled up with a $6.99 large one-topping from the pizza joint next door.

DAY 27

Even though we were heading towards one of our most anticipated destinations, leaving Missoula was difficult. Jim hadn't been back to his home town in quite some time, and I knew he wanted to see much more. But, we already had to make up time from our extended stay in Spokane. After a morning catching up on email and other work items, and a visit to the grocery store to pick up food for the next couple of days, we finally got on the road shortly after noon.

Sometimes when you're traveling you come across a place exactly when you need it. That was our next stop, although it wasn't immediately apparent.

Since we'd been on the road we'd seen little of the world except for what was right in front of us. Occasionally, like our waiting time at the Spokane Valley Firestone, we'd catch glimpses of atrocities. The rare times we checked social media we were inundated with people's anger. Camping and the isolation it provided was peaceful; motels and their wifi meant we could check in, which made me immediately want to check out.

People are good. I believe this. Being on the road and consistently encountering kindness and smiles reinforces that belief. But after checking in that morning and witnessing intolerance spewed like bison's offal, I needed some Zen.

North of Missoula is a place called Garden of 1000 Buddhas. It surprised Jim, not just because it didn't exist when he lived in Montana, but also because it's located near Arlee on the Flathead Indian Reservation. On most reservations, the land belongs to the sovereign nation. Flathead is different. The land belonged to the tribes after the 1855 Treaty of Hellgate, but in 1904, the U.S. Congress decided that whatever acreage wasn't specifically allotted to tribal members could be divvied up among homesteaders. The Confederated Salish and Kootenai, the tribal residents of Flathead, were given first choice of 80- and 160-acre plots and the rest was opened up to non-natives.

That's how a Buddhist monk came to purchase a sixty-acre sheep ranch in the middle of sacred lands. It could have been fodder for another clash of cultures, but the natives' new neighbor was a Buddhist, and his

goal for the new development was to spread world peace. Gochen Tulku Sang-ngag Rinpoche, the Tibetan lama who envisioned the garden, made it clear to the Confederated Salish and Kootenai Tribes that he knew he was their guest. Since the beginning, the tribes have participated in the garden's annual peace festival in addition to other ceremonies.

We entered the International Peace Garden through a grand gate that had been erected the year before. As I was crossing to the sidewalk from the parking area, a dusty gold Subaru sped so close to me I jumped, and it kicked up gravel as it raced towards the handicap spot. The car didn't have disabled plates, and as the woman exited and walked quickly towards the garden, I had to remind myself where we were.

Deep breaths, I told myself. "That lady obviously needs this place more than I do," I grumbled.

The Garden of 1000 Buddhas is peace in a valley. Whether you're Buddhist or not, all are welcome. A row of large charcoal gray monuments topped with spires, called stupas, paralleled the gravel road. We noticed there were gold carvings inside cavities in the sculptures. Smaller white stupas topped a wall that encircled a large figure atop a pedestal. The statue was of Yum Chenmo, who represents Transcendant Perfection of Wisdom. She's depicted as a woman because that wisdom is the mother of all Buddhas. Eight spokes of white radiated from the center, and each spoke was topped with 125 Buddhas, fulfilling the garden's name.

We walked around the dharma wheel, as it's called, and read quotes etched into boulders. We passed more sculptures and stopped at a pond decorated with tall grasses and colorful flowers. In the distance, prayer flags flapped atop a hill.

As we left, we encountered a woman with two young girls, one of whom strutted her style with an outfit of cowboy boots, a long skirt, and a sequined top. All three smiled and moved off the path to make sure they weren't blocking our photos. We smiled back and thanked them, and then walked back to Jeannie the Jeep.

Anger on the way in; kindness on the way out. Gee, Garden, could you get any more obvious?

At some point we'd get to Glacier National Park, but first we had to stop at the National Bison Range. As we neared the refuge, the distant snow-covered peaks disappeared behind mounds that looked like the sandhills of Nebraska. Right before we turned into the range, a lone bison stood atop one of those hills like a sentinel. We entered the park and could see the cragged mountains again. We were so close! But, when there's a National Bison Range on the way, and bison have dogged most of your trip, you go.

We drove slowly around the grasslands. The thing about wildlife refuges is that you're never guaranteed to actually see any wild animals. The whole idea is to give them room to roam. This range is home to a herd of between 325 and 350 bison, and we saw two or three and a couple of deer. That's OK, though. Those animals weren't there for our entertainment. Teddy Roosevelt set up the National Bison Range in 1908 to protect his beloved mammal, and more than a century later, it still does.

Glacier, here we come! It was nearly six o'clock when we drove through the gates, but I wasn't worried about securing a campsite. I'd been keeping an eye on the park's website, when I had access, and could see that Apgar Campground hadn't been filling up. Besides, it was a Monday, and for Glacier it was still fairly early in the season. In fact, we found out the Going-to-the-Sun Road, the major thoroughfare through the park, had only opened that past Saturday. Once again, our timing and luck held.

We picked out our site and while Jim set up our tent I rode my bike to the payment station. When I got back we drove to Apgar Village for some firewood and frosty treats. They'd sold out of huckleberry, but that was OK. Ice cream was ice cream in Montana. We strolled to the south shore of Lake McDonald and I licked my mint chocolate chip and said, "I feel like I'm home."

Lake McDonald in Glacier National Park

Frosty treats, clean mountain air, pine tree-cloaked slopes, a red boat bobbing in the clear blue water and sharp black peaks in the distance. What more could a gal want?

Back at the site, Jim started a fire and I made dinner. We ate around nine, the sun set at ten and soon, we slept.

DAY 28

The 28th day began like so many others had on this adventure. I woke up to the sounds of birds, pulled out the Coleman stove and my French press, and made coffee. It was our 14th day of camping; half of our nights had been spent outdoors. For a flash of a moment the day before I'd thought it would be nice to stay in the lodge, but that didn't last long. That morning, I laughed at the idea. There was nowhere else I'd rather be.

We had neighbors on both sides, but sitting at the table in a forest that nearly surrounded our tent, looking up at the mountain in front of me, it felt like it was just Jim and me. I broke out my computer to download photos and videos from my camera and smiled at the incongruity. I waited for the thousands of images I'd taken to transfer, knowing I'd add several hundred more from Glacier alone. We'd barely edged into the park, but from what I had seen I could tell it was going to be one heck of a day.

I forgot about the traumas in the world and reveled in the breeze. High up the mountain, one tree seemed to stand apart from the rest, and when the wind blew it waved like a queen in a parade. It was time to get out there and meet this royal landscape.

There's a short trail through the woods to the Apgar Visitor Center and we rode our bikes over after breakfast. We discovered they offered an audio tour of the Going-to-the-Sun Road, so we connected to their wifi and downloaded the files for the drive. We then followed our standard practice and asked the ranger what we should see in our limited time. She told us about a trail on the north side of Lake McDonald. We wheeled back to our site, locked up our bikes, and off we went.

Ever since we'd entered the western states, every time we talked to my father-in-law he'd ask me if I'd had enough "wows" yet. I told him I didn't think that was possible, and that was before Glacier National Park.

Wow. Wow wow wow.

We picked up the Going-to-the-Sun Road and drove around Lake McDonald, stopping once for a peek at the teal water. Like most of the lower-elevation lakes in this park, this one was carved by glaciers. It's deep, it's cold, and it's clear; the water never gets warmer than 50 degrees

Fahrenheit on the surface. That's too cold for plankton to survive, so the microorganisms aren't around to muddy things up.

The ranger had told us to follow North Lake McDonald Road and park just on the other side of the bridge. We squeezed Jeannie into the last space and grabbed our trekking poles. We wouldn't really need them, but we weren't sure how long or steep the hike would be. It was a nice, leisurely walk in the woods. At the end of the trail a transparent stream sailed over boulders and bubbled into a milky froth.

Always ask the rangers.

Glacier National Park

We got back on the road and every turn was another gasp, another wow. Occasionally we'd see evidence of previous wildfires, acres of stripped trees surrounded by fields of green. Everywhere we looked, waterfalls plunged. Sometimes they were in the distance, sometimes they plunged under the road, and the weeping wall flowed over the road. We were so in awe of everything around us that most of the time we flat out forgot about the audio tour.

Going-to-the-Sun Road is 53 miles. We wouldn't have time to drive the length of it, turn around, and come back, so our goal was Logan Pass and the Hidden Lake Overlook trail. The sign said the lot was full, but we

pulled in anyway and quickly found a spot. We were at the highest point of the road on the Continental Divide, in the ridges of the narrow backbone of the Rocky Mountains. Not far from where we stood, Triple Divide Peak diverted melting snow to the Atlantic, the Pacific, and the Arctic Oceans. In keeping with our center-of-everything theme, it's the hydrological apex of North America. Talk about being on top of the world.

Snow banks surrounded the Visitor Center. After a few feet along the slippery trails we debated going back to the car to get our trekking poles, because this time we'd opted to leave them behind. I also considered putting on the heavy-duty hiking boots I'd carted for 5,000 miles. Did I use either? Why, no, of course not. Instead, I decided to challenge myself on a trail packed with eight feet of snow in shoes with a barely existent tread. I thought slipping and sliding on a hike that started at 6,612 feet and had an elevation gain of 540 would be great fun.

We followed in the footprints of fellow hikers, learning quickly to try to place our feet in the depressions they'd left. I nearly lost my balance a few times and we climbed up, and up, and up. The trail skirted a slope; although the angle wasn't steep, it was a long way down.

Nearing the top of the first hill, we thought, "We're almost there!" We weren't.

If the snow didn't make the hike challenging, the wind would have. Brutal, capricious, it pushed from the sides and into our faces, never from the back. Closer to the overlook, the trees' branches extended on one side only, like they were clapping hands. Hikers coming back told us this time, yes, we were almost there. A mountain goat wandered through a grove. In places, the snow had melted and we walked on the boardwalk. It was like stepping off a rocking ship onto dry land. After almost a mile and a half, there it was. Hidden Lake. It stretched out below us, covered with snow and ice, Bearhat Mountain's black peak towering above.

It was still more than a mile to get to the lake itself and that trail was closed. We turned around, made our way back, and let oncoming trekkers know it wasn't too much further. I slipped; I slid. But I didn't fall. Until. We hit that slope and I went down on my derriere. I sat for a moment to get my breath. Then a lady decided to slide, standing up, down the path right next to me. I braced myself. If she fell, I was going down, down, down. She stumbled, caught herself, and ran further down the hill, gleefully laughing like a reckless crazy person. She had no idea she'd terrified the pants off of me, but her companion apologized as he went by. My temper had melted the snow enough that I was able to get a purchase on the trail while Jim helped me up.

Mountain Goat hanging out at the top of the world.

"Martini."

"You got it," he said.

By the time we got back to the parking lot, our 3-mile hike had taken two and a half hours. And every single minute of it, even the near-run-in with Miss Gleeful, was worth it. I had done something I didn't know I could do, and I felt amazing.

We skipped the overlooks on the way back because we knew we'd be driving the road the next day. On the way, we encountered a traffic jam, Glacier-style. Bighorn sheep blocked the road and there was nothing to do but wait. They finally meandered back up the hill and we continued towards Lake McDonald Lodge. By 6:30 we were sitting outside, listening to the water lap the shore and sipping cocktails.

There was a ranger program back at the campground that we wanted to catch. We drove to the other side of the lake, picked up a couple cones of frosty treats, and settled in to learn about Glacier National Park's geological history. The tops of the mountains are some of the oldest rock on earth and, she said, are one of the reasons the park's been designated a UNESCO World Heritage Site. At quarter 'til ten we finally sat down for dinner by the fire and then crawled into our tent. I went to bed depleted and smiling.

Wow.

Top - view from Going-to-the-Sun Road. Bottom - Hidden Lake

From Lake McDonald Lodge

HUCKLEBERRY! (and mint chocolate chip) ICE CREAM

DAY 29

If you're beginning to wonder if Jim and I are for real, I don't blame you. We sure sound happy, don't we? I've called him a saint. It's obvious we like each other and we still have fun together, even though by this point in the trip we'd spent nearly every moment - together. And not just together. TOGETHER. With the exception of our time in Spokane when we had family distractions, it had been 28 days of just the two of us. Jim and me. Noooobody else. All day. All night. Four weeks. And for much of that, we were together in a metal box with nowhere to go.

Did we fight? No. Yes. Sort of.

There were moments, especially in the beginning of the trip, when we'd get on each other's nerves. We were already stressed because we'd packed up our lives; what we didn't put into storage we took with us. Money was a factor. As entrepreneurs, we had the freedom to get up and go, but we couldn't actively pursue revenue, and we had to watch every expense. That's why we camped so frequently, ate trail mix and nut butter wraps for lunch, took advantage of $6.99 pizza nights, and sometimes stayed in crappy motels. Fortunately, we had no rent or mortgage, but that also meant we had no home and we didn't know how long it would take to find one.

Frankly, *I'm* amazed by us. We survived by knowing when to shut up, by choosing our battles wisely, and by reminding ourselves (frequently) what an incredible opportunity this was. For the most part, all was quiet on our western front. And then, on the 29th day...

We pulled into the parking lot for Apgar Visitor Center and suddenly we were sniping at each other and I was slamming Jeannie the Jeep's door and stomping off and sitting on a bench and glaring at all the happy people enjoying their day in this incredible place. Jim was off doing something else, most likely also glaring and silently fuming. But at some point, both of us realized that we could not do this. We *would* not do this. How often would we get to experience Glacier National Park? Neither one of us wanted to taint that memory with bitterness and anger, so we found each other and apologized.

Sometimes, it's that simple.

Tiff over, we resumed our journey with a little less tension. Before our mini-blow-up we didn't even realize we had been tense, but afterwards, we felt lighter. I'm not advising that anyone argue just to argue, but when you've been on your absolute best behavior for nearly a month, sometimes a slammed door and a "Well, yeah? You did THIS!" can help let off some steam. It did for us, anyway, and we got back on the Going-to-the-Sun Road with a renewed sense of calm. I'm sure it didn't hurt that we were in an International Peace Park.

Going-to-the-Sun Road

Glacier National Park shares a border with Canada's Waterton Lakes National Park. Like state borders, nature doesn't follow international divisions, so in 1931, members of Rotary International from Alberta and Montana proposed that the parks be united. The service-based club was fairly new, originating in Chicago in 1905, and 26 years later had spread to multiple chapters around the world. In 1932, the Rotarians' efforts succeeded and the two national parks joined to become Waterton-Glacier International Peace Park. Well, technically they're joined, but they're also still individual national parks and you need a passport to go from one to the other.

We didn't make it far enough north to meet our neighbor park. Our destination that night was Great Falls, Montana, so we drove straight through Glacier. "Straight" isn't accurate in the slightest. Although there's only one switchback, Going-to-the-Sun follows the curves and slopes of the Rocky Mountains as the road cuts from west to east. Like Needles, Beartooth, and Columbia River Highways, this was another phenomenal feat of engineering from the early 20th century. When we looked across the valleys and tried to pick out the narrow two-lane it practically blended into the scenery. Construction of the road took twenty years and three million dollars, and its completion in 1933 was heralded with speeches, music, and a performance of the Star Spangled Banner by the Blackfeet Tribal Band. We marveled at the road's excellent condition, especially considering the extreme weather it endures, as well as the number of vehicles that travel its length during a short time span each year.

The road served as a counterpoint to the riotous beauty that surrounded us. We stopped multiple times. When we crossed Logan Pass we noticed a bizarre cloud formation. It was smooth and flat: dark blue tinged with purple in the distance, a line of white like a toothpick had been dragged through it in the middle, and the colors faded to white and feathered into the blue above us. It looked ominous and freaky, especially with the sharp black mountains and the deep green forest.

And we were driving towards it.

We kept going and the sun held. We saw what remained of Jackson

Glacier, the teal of St. Mary's Lake, and the peaks of St. Mary Visitor Center before driving onto the Blackfeet Indian Reservation and under the clouds.

Those clouds might have looked like harbingers of doom, but once we were under them they made for just another gray day. It didn't even rain.

Four hours after leaving Glacier we pulled into the O'Haire Motor Inn. This motel was our sole reason for visiting Great Falls. Why?

Mermaids.

The O'Haire Motor Inn has a bar, and that bar is called the Sip-n-Dip Lounge, and it's called the Sip-n-Dip because you can see into the motel pool while you're sitting at the bar. The lounge opened in 1962 during the height of the tiki bar craze, and while most of those bars sank, the Sip-n-Dip stayed afloat. Why? Who knows? It could have been the appeal of bamboo decor and tropical drinks in a place known for thunderstorms and long, cold winters. It might be because of Piano Pat, a legend who's been crooning in her distinctive, ahem, style, at the lounge since 1963. Since the mid-90s, it might be because of the mermaids. Up until that time, bar patrons might be treated to the sight of motel guests doing laps or swimming in their floaties. But then bar manager Sandra Johnson-Thares included a mermaid in one year's New Year's Eve festivities; once you've had mermaids in Montana, there's no going back.

It's kitschy, sure, but it works. I mean, we went to Great Falls, Montana, and I booked a room at the O'Haire Motor Inn just so we could sit at the bar and wave to mermaids.

I always did like dive bars.

(You just groaned, didn't you?)

At first one lady bobbed behind the glass. She'd wave at the people lined up at the bar sipping beers and fish bowls, and used hand signs to chat with a man who brought a mermaid puppet. After a bit she was joined by another woman in a fin, and the two tossed plastic fish, blew bubbles, and did other mermaid-type things.

The bar was packed when we arrived, but a couple of spots opened and we moved to the front row. We ended up next to Cody, a man who visited Great Falls frequently for business. The three of us chatted while Piano Pat played Margaritaville and delivered "searching for my lost shaker of salt...salt...salt..." like a gravely spoken word poem. It was performance art defined. Cody told us about an Irish bar that offered its entire list of whiskeys and scotches for half-price on Wednesdays, and lo and behold, guess what day it was! We sauntered a few blocks to the pub, sipped a pair of Balvenie 12-year Doublewood for $13 total. After overhearing someone say, "And they don't allow goat traffic" (we had no idea what that meant, either), we decided to sashay back to the motel.

DAY 30

We began our day with breakfast at Clark and Lewie's Pub and Grill, the restaurant inside the O'Haire Motor Inn. Great Falls, Montana, is officially Lewis and Clark country. As in, they were HERE, Lewis and Clark country. The Mandan, a hospitable tribe in what is now Washburn, North Dakota, had warned the explorers about the series of waterfalls in this stretch of the Missouri River and that it would cause a delay in their travels. Meriwether Lewis scouted ahead of the rest of the Corps of Discovery with one companion and the two reached the great falls on June 13, 1805. Lewis recounted the event in his journal. His spelling may have been rather fluid, but the name of his companion is quite clear:

"I had proceed on this course about two miles with Goodrich at some distance behind me whin my ears were saluted with the agreeable sound of a fall of water and advancing a little further I saw the spray arrise above the plain like a collumn of smoke which soon began to make a roaring too tremendious to be mistaken for any cause short of the great falls of the Missouri."

There was a Goodrich in the Corps of Discovery! Private Silas Goodrich from Massachusetts loved fishing and excelled at it. He caught several blackspotted cutthroat trout in the Missouri River the day he and Lewis found the falls. It was the first time anyone in the expedition had seen that type of fish, so the explorers preserved samples. The fish's scientific name is *Oncorhynchus clarkii lewisi* to honor the explorers. In 1977, the fish that Goodrich found was declared the official state fish. See? Goodriches are good for Montana.

Mermaids may have brought us to Great Falls, but we couldn't leave without a visit to the Lewis and Clark Historic Trail Interpretive Center. It's located just east of Upper Pitch, the last in the series of five falls that forced them to portage for eighteen and a quarter miles. That portage cost them a month, and it was at this location that they accepted they would not make it to the Pacific Ocean and back in one year. This was also where they came together as a cohesive unit, realizing if they didn't work together, they'd never survive.

In addition to those details, we also learned that it sometimes took five different people to translate so the explorers could converse with native peoples. Their most famous interpreter became a legend. Sacagawea (or Sakakawea) was part of the Corps of Discovery, but not as a guide as I learned in school. Her husband, Toussaint Charbonneau, was a French Canadian fur-trader, and when he joined the expedition, Sacagawea and their infant child joined, too. Born to the Shoshone tribe, the young woman had been kidnapped in 1800 by the Hidatsa and then sold to Charbonneau. She was probably about seventeen when the three joined the Corps.

Her ability to interpret with the Shoshone, which helped secure horses for the expedition's mountain passage, proved to be invaluable. Charbonneau, Sacagawea, and their child traveled nearly the entire journey, leaving the explorers only when they returned to the Mandan village on the way back east.

The Interpretive Center is cleverly organized. Visitors begin by learning about President Jefferson's instructions to Lewis and Clark, and then travel through exhibits about the various tribes the explorers would have met: Otoe, Sioux, Mandan, Hidatsa, Shoshone, Salish, Nez Perce, Clatsop, Blackfeet, and Crow. Outside is a nature walk along the Missouri River. The river seemed calm enough to ford, but that's because the Black Creek Dam now controls the flow in that section.

We skipped the walk. We had a long drive ahead of us.

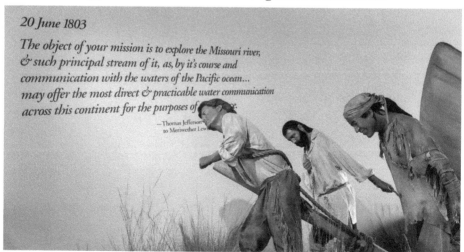

Jefferson's instructions to Lewis & Clark

I knew this day was coming. Jim had warned me: driving across central Montana requires commitment. It's not something you do unless you're properly fortified with snacks, have a full tank of gas, and know where you're going to sleep for the night. We filled the tank and we still had trail mix left from the giant bucket I'd made for just this reason, so we were good on those two accounts. I also had the presence of mind to book a hotel room before we left O'Haire Motor Inn, so we lit out for the east end of the state fully stocked and completely prepared. If only the weather would hold out.

After three solid hours on the road we pulled into a rest area. It was about halfway between Great Falls and Glendive, and we'd seen three trucks, a combine, and a bizarre art installation. That's what I'm calling it, anyway. A scarecrow rode a hay bale, rodeo-style, in the back of an ancient green pickup truck. It was pointed towards a dead tree that looked like Tim Burton had gotten ahold of it, with a face plastered on the trunk and curved wires capped with what looked like snake puppets. Bizarre.

It was just Jim and me at the rest stop. No cars passed or pulled in. The only sounds were a cow calling in the distance and birds. Inside, speakers broadcast the weather.

Uh-oh.

We'd had extremely good luck the last four weeks, skirting some nasty stuff and, with the exception of a couple of nights of rain and some

cloudy weather, had sailed under blue skies. This day, though, it looked like our luck might run out. The broadcast reported severe storms rolling in, so we got back into Jeannie the Jeep and pulled up the weather on her dashboard.

Double uh-oh.

On the screen, a block of red warned us that a huge storm was nipping at our bumper. In front of us was a huge yellow area that included our destination. The speed limit on MT 200 was seventy, so we did that and a bit more in our hurry to get to shelter. We could see the downpour in the distance. About an hour out of Glendive the clouds boiled, just like the witch's cauldron we'd seen in Nebraska. We found out later that it was almost exactly like that formation. Once again, we'd escaped tornadoes.

By the time we got to our Days Inn the skies had calmed. We had no desire to push our luck, so we ordered Chinese, had it delivered to our room, and finished that long day with perfect hot and sour soup in a small town in eastern Montana.

DAY 31

Don't underestimate small towns.

It's something I've learned over and over. It's something I've preached over and over. Yet here we were in a small town in eastern Montana, and I thought we'd be there to sleep and leave.

Have I learned nothing?

When we approached our hotel the night before we'd noticed signs for both a dinosaur museum and a frontier museum. Inside the hotel, a bunch of tourism brochures were piled next to the Chinese takeout menu. I resist visitor guides and flyers about as well as I do perfect hot and sour soup, so I grabbed a few that looked interesting. One of those brochures was for the largest state park in Montana. Our new plan was to visit two museums and the park and then we'd be back on the road.

We tried to visit the dinosaur museum. It looked pretty cool; the head of a T-Rex leapt out of the three-story windowless building. That museum wasn't open yet and we went next door to a squat building painted with murals.

We parked on the white gravel and found the Frontier Gateway Museum. Inside, Fayette greeted us from behind the counter and asked us if we'd been next door to the dinosaur museum. We told her we hadn't. "It's a creationism museum. They have beautiful displays." She paused. "Enough said."

Fayette gave us a "Museum Madness" bracket, an elimination tournament of historical items, and we ticked which artifacts we thought should make it to the next level. Would it be the fire engine or the petrified fire carrier? The Iron Lung or Margie the Dinosaur? A razor used in a crime, or a fire chain? It was a brilliant device that made us pay attention and focus on the exhibits. There was no map to tell us where we could find each item, so we had to search everywhere, including the extensive outdoor displays.

This was a community museum, which meant many of the items were donated by people who had either used them or knew the people who had. It infused the displays with meaning. Somebody in Glendive knew somebody who used that cash register, or wore that hat, or broke a story on that typewriter. It was the best of community historical repositories, a compendium of eastern Montana from prehistoric eras to more recent times.

We skipped the fauxseum next door, choosing to visit Montana's largest state park instead. Makoshika is a variant of the Lakota's *mako sica -*

The Badlands of Eastern Montana - Makoshika State Park

bad lands. It's a landscape of erosion, and *Triceratops* and *Tyrannosaurus rex* fossils have been found in its exposed history. We drove the main road in the park, noting the disc golf course at the entrance and the radio towers at the top of a hill. At one overlook, a picnic table edged just to the rim. Pine and juniper grew where they could. In some places, the mesas had layers stacked one upon another, as defined as a picnic pie. Capstone rocks looked for all the world like giant enoki mushrooms. Our unplanned visit to Glendive had turned into quite the surprise. But, I suppose we should have expected that.

We entered North Dakota. As soon as we got to Medora and had cell service I needed to extend our rental of Jeannie the Jeep for a couple of days. It was Friday and she was due back on Monday. We could make it, but we'd be pushing and wouldn't be able to see anything of Minnesota or Wisconsin and very little of North Dakota. Even with an extension, we still had a lot of ground to cover. I called Hertz to extend our rental.

They said no.

It wasn't because they needed the vehicle. It was because Jeannie needed an oil change.

"We did that in Spokane," I told them. Didn't matter; corporate said local had put the hold on because they didn't have a record of the maintenance, even though Hertz had paid for it. We talked to local. She needed a copy of the receipt. I took a picture of it and emailed it to her. It had to be a PDF.

I was standing in a parking lot in the historic town of Medora, North Dakota, mere yards away from Theodore Roosevelt National Park. "Can't you talk to accounting? Firestone?" No. She needed a PDF copy of the receipt.

Balderdash.

"I can't do this right now," I thought. Jim and I decided to take a quick walk around the town, enter the national park, and he would call the next day. I'm a fierce do-it-myself person, but when it comes to customer service, it's best for everyone involved if Jim handles it. His deep, smooth voice, calming demeanor, and years as an IT help desk manager mean that he can navigate the most infuriating bureaucracies with dignity, whereas I turn into a screeching banshee. It is not one of my finer qualities. If we had to have Jeannie back on Monday, so be it, but we were in Medora and we were going to enjoy it.

It's a small, small town. And by small, I mean miniscule. It's .37 square miles with a population of 112. We walked around most of it, popped into a gift shop to look for hats and took a picture with a statue of Teddy.

Maltese Cross Cabin

Bison crossing the Little Missouri River

We debated on getting some frosty treats, but decided we better get a move on. As it was, our visit to Theodore Roosevelt National Park was almost painfully short. We briefly toyed with the idea of camping, but with our vehicle situation unresolved, decided it would be better to get as far east as we could.

We browsed the visitor center and stepped into the Maltese Cross Cabin. That cabin had traveled more than most people at the time. It began life as the future president's ranch cabin in 1883. Once Roosevelt became president, the cabin became an exhibit at the World's Fair in St. Louis and the Lewis and Clark Centennial Exposition in Portland, both in 1905. A few years later it was on the state fairgrounds in West Fargo, and then it moved to the state capitol grounds in Bismarck. In 1959, the log cabin was moved one final time to Theodore Roosevelt National Park.

We drove about half of the scenic drive, passing wild horses (horsies!) grazing at the top of a hill. A short hike on the Wind Canyon Trail and we were overlooking a horseshoe bend of the Little Missouri River. Off to the left a herd of bison waded into the muddy water to get to the other side. It was nearly four in the afternoon. We turned around and drove back to the entrance, stopping at another prairie dog farm. As we passed the cottonwood-covered campground, I felt a tug of sadness. I was afraid this

would be our last opportunity to hike and sleep outdoors, and we had to skip it because we needed to cover some ground.

It was close to nine when we rolled into Jamestown on the other side of the state. We found a local place and shared fried pickles, seasoned fries, and a shredded beef sandwich loaded with gloppy yellow cheese. It was glorious.

DAY 32

E verything looks better in the morning.

Jim called Hertz and extended our rental. With his mellifluous tones, empathy, and patience, our problem was solved and we had some breathing room. We had to be back by July 3, but that was four days away and those two extra days meant everything.

We checked out of our motel and laughed as we walked back from the office. Parked next to Jeannie the Jeep was a white pick-up truck emblazoned with "Miss Rodeo North Dakota" and a likeness of her face. Jim realized we'd seen her in the breakfast line, so now we'd met (sort of) two rodeo queens.

We were in Jamestown, North Dakota, because it's the home of the National Buffalo Museum and the World's Largest Buffalo Monument. You might have noticed I've been calling these giant animals bison. Technically, that's what they are, but for a couple hundred years the colloquial term for them was buffalo. American buffalo, to be exact. The issue with the name "buffalo" is that there's already an animal in Asia called the water buffalo, and the American mammal is a different species. It's kind of like calling almond milk, "milk."

The museum educates on the importance of bison to the indigenous peoples, and how an animal that numbered in the millions could be reduced to near extinction in the span of less than a century. In 1800, 40 to 60 million bison roamed the plains. In 1889, only 541 remained.

Some reduction in numbers should be expected with an increased population, but the bison's near destruction was calculated. The animals provided food, clothing, and shelter for the Native Americans, and without them, the people would struggle. Knowing this, after the Civil War wiping out the bison became part of the U.S. Army's strategy to defeat the tribes.

With the slaughter came a new, albeit short-lived, industry. All of those dead animals left tons of bones, and people would collect them in piles by railroad depots. They'd then be shipped to factories where they could be used to create industrial carbon and fertilizer. But then those were gone, too.

Fortunately, wiser heads stopped the bison from being completely exterminated. Walking Coyote raised six orphaned bison on Montana's Flathead Reservation. In 1894, President Grover Cleveland signed a bill into law that protected the American buffalo. In 1896, at the urging of his wife, Charles Goodnight began breeding them in his Texas ranch and sent some to the New York Zoological Society, which is now the Bronx Zoo. We saw a few of their descendants in Oklahoma on our previous cross-country trip. By the early 1900s, the American Buffalo Society, of which Teddy Roosevelt was honorary president, began establishing buffalo ranges. Gradually, the numbers increased, and now there are about half a million bison in public and private ranges.

Outside the museum in a fenced glade, a small herd roamed and a white bull stood on his own. This was Dakota Miracle, offspring of the legendary White Cloud, an albino buffalo that's preserved inside the museum. White buffalo are considered sacred by some Native Americans, and the presence of these rare creatures brings more visitors to the museum

and to Jamestown. Drawing tourists to the area was the goal behind the construction of Dakota Thunder, the World's Largest Buffalo Monument. Chamber of Commerce President Harold Newman had the idea for the 60-ton behemoth, and by 1959 it was beckoning travelers.

Worked for us.

To get to the monument we walked through Frontier Village, but that's all we had time to do. A Nordic runestone was calling my name.

World's Largest Buffalo

In 1898, a Swedish immigrant named Olof Ohman made a remarkable discovery in rural Minnesota. He'd recently acquired some new land and was clearing stumps and trees so he could farm it when he came across a heavy stone entangled in the roots of a poplar tree. This wasn't just any stone; etchings covered the surface. Olof discovered they were runes, the ancient written language of his homeland. Translated, these runes seemed to indicate that Scandinavians had made it to Minnesota in the year 1362.

What were the chances? Many said it was nigh well impossible. In other words, they thought Mr. Ohman's story and his runestone were a bunch of bunk. There were a few reasons for this. To the skeptics, it seemed conveniently coincidental that Olof, who had arrived in Minnesota in 1890, would find proof that his countrymen had been in the same area five hundred years before he'd arrived. When he found the stone, Leif Ericson was a hot topic and it was a few short years after Norway had sent a replica Viking ship to the World's Columbian Exposition in Chicago. Plus, the translation seemed off, and six linguists and historians declared the runestone a hoax.

Others, however, believe the Kensington Runestone, named for the town closest to where Olof found the stone, is authentic. The museum is founded on that belief, and there are several displays showcasing the extensive scientific research done in recent years.

Of course, one of the biggest questions is whether it's even possible, and the Runestone Museum makes a compelling argument that it is.

The museum is in Alexandria, about twenty miles from Olaf's discovery. In addition to the infamous stone, there are displays about pioneer life and the original inhabitants. Outside are historical buildings and a barn that's jam-packed with miscellany, including a replica of a Viking merchant ship. And, an open one-horse sleigh.

Across the street from the museum is "Big Ole, the largest Viking in the land." He's been welcoming visitors to Alexandria since 1965, when he accompanied the runestone to the New York World's Fair.

We took our obligatory photo and drove to Eden Prairie on the outskirts of Minneapolis. We'd hoped to get a little further, but hotels were cheaper around the city. Besides, we'd already driven more than 350 miles that day and spent six and a half hours in the car. Eden Prairie would do just fine.

DAY 33

"**I** love the big puffy clouds," I said, "when they're not dropping stuff."

I'd officially hit the loopy stage. That's OK. We were getting closer to "home" with every mile. In two more days we'd be back in Illinois and then we could rest.

BWAHAHAHAHAHA! Oh, my. Anyway... Day 33's agenda was light. We drove through Owatonna so I could see a Louis Sullivan-designed jewel box. It was built in 1908 as the National Farmers' Bank of Owatonna and it's now a Wells Fargo. Since it was Sunday I couldn't go inside, but that gorgeous red brick exterior with green terra cotta and stained glass windows was worth the quick detour.

The only other item on our list was SPAM®. There is a SPAM® Museum in Austin, Minnesota. I think if I had decided to skip this palace of pork, everyone who knows me, including you (because you know me by now), would be disappointed. SPAM® is one of those polarizing foods that

people love to love or love to hate. It's the cilantro of canned meats.

SPAM® has quite the history. Hormel first produced it in 1937, which proved to be good timing for both the company and U.S. soldiers. More than 150 million pounds of the preserved pork product were shipped to the front, which is how it landed in Hawaii, Guam, and the Philippines. The museum has a whole room showing how this product has supported and continues to support the troops. There are lots of interactive exhibits, a section just for kids, and screens of recipes showing the various ways you can use SPAM® in your menu. We also learned what's in those rectangular cans. Surprisingly, it's just six ingredients: pork with ham, salt, water, sugar, potato, and sodium nitrate. If you want a little more flavor they've got jalapeno, black pepper, chorizo, teriyaki, and other varieties.

A friend of ours lives near Austin and she met us for lunch. The museum doesn't have a cafe, so we found a restaurant a block away that had a whole SPAM® menu. We shared chorizo SPAM® quesadillas and Philly SPAM® and Cheese. Both were surprisingly tasty, and I felt better knowing the meat was actually meat and wasn't just a tin full of chemicals as I'd assumed. Teach me to not look at labels.

We left Austin, drove towards the Mississippi River, crossed it, and entered Wisconsin. It was 7:30 when we checked in to our hotel in Onalaska, and I was in bed by 7:45. Two more days.

DAY 34

Home. That's what I felt as we rode our bikes on the Great River State Trail. Home. I loved the unrestrained and extreme beauty of the west, the sheer extravagance of the earth's upheaval, the power of an ever-changing landscape. It was one "wow" after another. But as we rode our bikes along the Mississippi River on a flat path through leafy trees that would be bare by November, I was home.

Jim looking none too happy that I'm taking a selfie while riding

I'd grown up in the Midwest and had lived in Indiana or Illinois all but four years of my life. Jim and I camped on our honeymoon just a few miles up the river, and on our one-year anniversary about fifty miles south. This was a land I knew.

We were close enough that we could have ended our journey that day, but we knew we weren't done yet. We followed another two lane, stopped at more historical markers. Learned about rural electrification and farm boys finding mastadon bones in rural Wisconsin. Jim noticed a field of flags and we stopped at American Legion Post 13 to pay our respects.

It was only one in the afternoon when we found our spot in Governor Dodge State Park. July 2, and we practically had the place to ourselves. We set up our tent one last time and drove to Dodgeville in search of some food. There wasn't much open, but we did find a Mexican restaurant. Jim had a quesadilla; I had a tostada and an enchilada. We picked up some Spotted Cow, a beer you can only get in Wisconsin, and were back in our campsite by five. He started a fire and I read *The Full English* by author and friend Bull Garlington. I'd laugh out loud every few minutes and Jim finally stopped asking "What?" after the gazillionth time I told him "Oh, nothing. Bull ate more beans."

We spotted fireflies. These were sparks of my childhood, but Jim didn't have those memories. Fireflies don't live in Missoula.

I feel like I should say more. But that was it. That was our day. I suppose that's the danger in organizing a book by day. Some chapters are thousands of words. Others say simply "I napped." This day, I was home.

HOME

Almost. I should say *almost* home. Technically, we were still in Wisconsin and needed to get to Illinois. If you wanted to get truly technical, we still had no home at all.

Whatever. We were close.

We took our time breaking down camp that morning. We tried to take a hike, but we got about a hundred feet into it and said, "yeah, nope." Before we walked back those hundred feet, we watched the fastest butterfly we've ever seen. There was a concession stand and we had one more frosty treat. While we dipped into our black cherry chocolate chip, we watched a dad take his sobbing boy to the stand to replace a dropped scoop. On the way out of the park, we took a short walk to one more waterfall. The sun hit the cascading stream just right and its white reflection led a path directly to us. We said Yes, one more time.

Mineral Point was on the way. It's the most Cornwall you can get outside of England, but when we visited, not much was open. That was fine. I was happy to browse the buffet of National Historic Register markers as we walked uphill and down. Rainbow flags and artist boutiques let me know this was a place I'd like to visit in depth. Some other time.

We stayed on the two-lanes as long as we could stand it, but after a while we were done. Our trip was done. Now it was all about unloading what we could into our storage unit, picking up our car, and returning Jeannie the Jeep.

Dropping the keys into the return box felt like saying goodbye to a friend. If the office had been open, I would have asked, "How much to keep her?" But, it was after hours on July 3, so we deposited her keys and checked into our room at the Holiday Inn. We'd stay there for two nights and then house sit for a couple of weeks while we looked for a place to live. (In case you're wondering, we found one, and it was worth the drama.)

The next day we celebrated our country's independence with friends. I'm afraid we weren't terribly good company. Both of us were shell-shocked, and would be for some time.

We had driven 6,832.9 miles, visited twelve states, and spent 166.58 hours - nearly seven days - in the car. At dinner, our friends asked us our favorite places and experiences, and we looked at each other for guidance. There was no favorite. There was no "best." There's a string of memories and each is unique. Picking a favorite is nebulous swipes at a pinata.

We had seen...I don't know how to describe what we saw besides what I've already written. Over and over we encountered kindness. Rarely, we met people who needed a lesson in empathy. But for the most part? We trusted that things would work out, that people would point us in the right direction, and that people are good. It did; they did; they are.

For the second time in two years, Jim and I turned off the noise and drove, and it was, again, the best time of our lives.

So far.

ACKNOWLEDGEMENTS

Writing my first book was hard. The second? Harder. Fortunately, I'm lucky enough to have some pretty incredible people in my corner. Although the act of writing is solitary, I certainly didn't do this alone.

Thank you, first and foremost, to Jim. Your patience, your humor, your willingness to take these adventures, and your mad driving skills make this possible. I love you more than I love horsies.

Thank you, Mom and Dad, for your constant love, support and (relatively) unbiased feeback. I'll never get tired of making you proud.

To Mom and Dad Goodrich, thank for the many places you suggested, for exploring with us for a bit, and for the constant love.

This book would be much less if it weren't for you, Tatiana. I've said it before: you make me a better writer, and your compassion makes me a better person.

If it weren't for Heidi Kohz, I couldn't have been present during this journey. Thank you, dear friend, for womanning the ship while I was away.

Cheryl, Tosch, Uncle John, the aunts - you infused this journey with meaning. I'm grateful to be part of the family and to have had the opportunity to meet you. And your fields, your alpacas, and your horsies.

Cliff and Lori - thank you for owning a cabin on the side of a mountain by a lake. And, more importantly, for being friends. It's pretty cool when you *want* to spend time with your in-laws.

Thank you, Sean, for being a wonderful son and for keeping the cat alive - again.

Thank you to Kristy for introducing us to your South Dakota relatives and your wonderful Aunt Alice, and thank you to the Marrs family for welcoming us into your home.

Thank you to Mark and Bob of Brown Street Inn, Kate from Visit Spokane, Clarissa from Think Iowa City, Betsy's Best Nut Butters, and Elizabeth from GrowlerWerks. We had better experiences, tasty snacks, and cold beer because of you.

I also want to thank Gretchen M. Garrison for her book, *Detour*

Nebraska, and Megan Bannister for her website, olioiniowa.com. Through their publications, both of these fellow Midwest Travel Network members introduced us to some of our favorite destinations.

Thank you, also, to everyone who cheered me on as I shared my excitement, fear, frustration, and glee during this process. You kept me going!

Finally, thank you, dear reader! I'm grateful you've chosen to read this adventure. I hope it inspires you to travel this big, wide, beautiful country. And if you aren't able to do that, then I hope you feel like you've shared these experiences with us.

THANK YOU!!!

ABOUT THE AUTHOR

Theresa L. Goodrich is an Emmy-winning author and content creator with a penchant for storytelling and a keen eye. She's the founder and publisher of The Local Tourist and author of the Two Lane Gems book series. Theresa has appeared in Crain's Chicago, and the Chicago Tribune, and on WGN, WLUP, ArcLight Connects, and WCIU. She was one of the founding bloggers of ChicagoNow, was the Chicago Expert for Answers.com, and is a contributor to multiple travel outlets. She's also spoken on marketing, motivation, entrepreneurship, writing, and (of course) travel.

You can follow Theresa at thelocaltourist.com and theresalgoodrich.com.